PARDON

My FRENCH

PARDON

My FRENCH

Unleash Your Inner Gaul

CHARLES TIMONEY

GOTHAM BOOKS

GOTHAM BOOKS
Published by Penguin Group (USA) Inc.
375 Hudson Street, New York, New York 10014, U.S.A.
Penguin Group (Canada), 90 Eglinton Avenue East, Suite 700, Toronto, Ontario
M4P 2Y3, Canada (a division of Pearson Penguin Canada Inc.); Penguin Books
Ltd, 80 Strand, London WC2R 0RL, England; Penguin Ireland, 25 St Stephen's
Green, Dublin 2, Ireland (a division of Penguin Books Ltd); Penguin Group
(Australia), 250 Camberwell Road, Camberwell, Victoria 3124, Australia (a
division of Pearson Australia Group Pty Ltd); Penguin Books India Pvt Ltd,
11 Community Centre, Panchsheel Park, New Delhi – 110 017, India; Penguin
Group (NZ), 67 Apollo Drive, Rosedale, North Shore 0632, New Zealand (a
division of Pearson New Zealand Ltd); Penguin Books (South Africa) (Pty) Ltd,
24 Sturdee Avenue, Rosebank, Johannesburg 2196, South Africa

Penguin Books Ltd, Registered Offices: 80 Strand,
London WC2R 0RL, England

First published in Great Britain in 2007 by Penguin UK

Published by Gotham Books, a member of Penguin Group (USA) Inc.

First printing, May 2008
1 3 5 7 9 10 8 6 4 2

Copyright © 2008 by Charles Timoney
All rights reserved

Gotham Books and the skyscraper logo are
trademarks of Penguin Group (USA) Inc.

LIBRARY OF CONGRESS CATALOGING-IN-PUBLICATION DATA

Timoney, Charles.
Pardon my French: unleash your inner Gaul / Charles Timoney.
p. cm.
ISBN 978-1-592-40373-8 (hardcover) I. France—Description and travel.
2. French language. 3. National characteristics, French. I. Title.
DC29.3.T56 2008
306.0944—dc22   2007046189

Printed in the United States of America
Set in Granjon
Designed by Spring Hoteling

While the author has made every effort to provide accurate telephone numbers and
Internet addresses at the time of publication, neither the publisher nor the author
assumes any responsibility for errors, or for changes that occur after publication.
Further, the publisher does not have any control over and does not assume any
responsibility for author or third-party Web sites or their content.

FOR INÈS, SARAH, AND SEBASTIAN

Contents

$\mathcal{I}$NTRODUCTION

It is only fair to point out, right from the beginning, that I am English. I think that this is something you should be aware of as early as possible in order to get the most out of this book.

For, while the book is an entertaining and informative view of France and French culture, it may also give you a good insight into the way English people see things. When you read it, you will quickly see that many of the definitions and descriptions have a particularly English slant to them.

I came to write this book because about twenty years ago my wife and I were both laid off in the same month. At the time, we were living in England where I was a patent attorney protecting the inventions of the company I worked for. Losing our jobs in the same month seemed to me to be disastrous. My wife, who is French, saw things differently and tried to get me to realize that this was a sign that we should leave England and go and live for a while in her native France.

So, in a moment of weakness, I agreed to apply for a job in Paris. The idea, at least for me, was to spend just a year or so there as an adventure in the hope that it would look good on my CV.

Having got the job (the fact that I was the only candidate may well have been a contributing factor), the main problem I was faced with over the first months was a staggering lack of useful French vocabulary. My new job was for the Paris division of a large U.S. company so the work that I did was all in English. However, I obviously needed to talk to my colleagues, and deal with day-to-day living, in French. I had studied the language for several years through school, but it became frighteningly clear from the very first morning at work that this was far from enough. My colleagues consistently used a wide variety of impenetrable slang and persisted in the annoying habit of talking about things I had never heard of.

Conversations tended to go too fast for me to be able to ask for explanations so I spent most of my early months in France in a painful haze of incomprehension. I am convinced that I would have had a chance of following at least some of what was going on if only I had known one or two key words. Surely, if you know that people are talking about secondhand cars, or income tax, or even gift wrap, you will have more chance of keeping up.

It seems likely that many visitors, whether English or American, who spend time in France must have the same sort of experience. So, in order to give you, whatever your level of French, a better chance of following what people are talking about, making sense of what you see in the street—or even of increasing your chances of leafing through a French newspaper and triumphantly thinking, "Oh! I've heard of that!"—I have made a selection of the various words that would certainly have made my life a lot easier had I known them when I first started work here all those years ago.

The words have been chosen to be as useful as possible and to give you a broad understanding of French life: they are not words that you probably learned at school, nor are the definitions the sort of thing you find in most dictionaries.

I have grouped them by themes such as Food, Travel, Entertainment, and the like. Even if you don't manage to remember them all, the definitions should provide a useful insight into what is really what in France.

Food and Drink

Where else could one start but with food and drink? One of the main reasons why so many people come on holiday to France is to take full advantage of both bars and restaurants.

But are you sure that you are ordering the right thing when you stop for a drink in a café? Are you getting the best value from your boulanger? *And what would you think if someone appeared to be asking you for a duck?*

You will also discover a variety of French dishes, find reassurance about whether they'd ever include horse meat, and get some useful advice about tipping.

Drinks *and* Cafés

APÉRO: *Apéro* is the familiar form of the word *apéritif* and it is definitely an important word to learn early on. With luck, you will encounter *un apéro* either at work or at home. At work, people seem to treat their colleagues to an aperitif before a meal to celebrate the birth of a baby, the buying of a new car, or to announce a change of job. I have fond memories of sitting down for lunch with colleagues whereupon one would rub his hands together with delight and cry, *"Allez! C'est moi qui vous offre l'apéro aujourd'hui!"* before going on to announce some especially good news. We also had a system where if you lost a bet, you had to pay for the *apéros* for everyone. You can of course have aperitifs away from the office, whether before a meal at home with friends or at a restaurant. Inviting someone for an *apéro* or, more correctly, inviting them to *venir prendre l'apéritif* is a pleasant and simpler alternative to inviting them to supper. The key element of a decent *apéro* is good sparkling wine, or preferably Champagne, in generous quantities. The ultimate *apéro*, which can rival a meal, is something called an *apéritif dinatoire*. If you get invited for

such an *apéro* you can expect the drinks to be accompanied by several different types of hot food and there should
even be something sweet at the end. Depending on how
much food is served, an *apéritif* can last anywhere from an
hour to all evening.

Bière: On one of my first forays into a pub with friends
at the tender age of sixteen, my friend Paul called for "a
half a pint of beer, please." This was met with hoots of
derision from the bartender; in England, because of the
different types available, you have to specify which sort
of beer—bitter, brown ale, mild, etc.—you actually want.
For once, things in France are simpler than in England,
for you can go into a French bar and order *une bière s'il
vous plaît* without running the risk of being humiliated.
The barman or waiter will generally ask for details, suggesting *une pression*, which means draft beer, or quoting a
few bottled beers that you might like to choose from. Experience suggests that the list of beers tends to start with
the cheapest and work upward. You can speed things up
by calling at the outset for *un demi*, which will lead to
the barman bringing a glass of draft beer straight away.
Un demi used to mean "half a liter" but now refers to
twenty-five cc or a quarter of a liter. Occasionally, you
still hear older men in bars calling for *un bock* when they
don't want to drink a whole *demi*. *Un bock* is a wineglass
of beer, roughly half the quantity of a *demi*. I don't know
anyone who drinks *bocks* as there is barely enough for a
single swallow.

CANARD: First of all, you should never offer French people granulated sugar with their coffee. If they are polite, they will be visibly shocked: if they are normal, they will react as though you were trying to poison them. Only sugar lumps should ever be offered with coffee in France. Having established this, the presence of sugar lumps in close proximity to coffee leads to one of the many excellent reasons for going to France: dunking sugar lumps in strong, black coffee is absolutely wonderful. The act of dunking a sugar lump, preferably a large, oblong one, in a cup of coffee is known as *faire un canard* where *canard*, as you know, normally means "duck." It is quite common, when several people are gathered around cups of coffee, for a person who hasn't asked for their own cup to pick up a sugar lump and lean over toward someone else's cup, asking, *"Je peux faire un canard?"* One can thus get a kick of sugary caffeine without having to drink a whole cup.

CHAMPAGNE: Champagne is sufficiently important in France to merit two special verbs that cover opening it and drinking it. For a start, you don't just say, *"On va boire du Champagne"* because it would make it sound about as festive as drinking tap water. When people speak about drinking generous quantities of Champagne, they use the verb *sabler* as, for example, *"Ce soir, on va sabler le Champagne."* *Sabler* doesn't mean "open" nor yet just "drink" but it means "to drink a good lot of Champagne on a festive occasion." There is also a really good word for opening a bottle of Champagne. This is *sabrer*. Even though

the words look similar, they are quite different. *Sabrer*
literally means "to cut with a saber." Thus *sabrer le Champagne* means to whack the neck of the bottle with a saber
and so dispense with all that fiddling with the twisted
wires. It is still used, even when no one is intending to
get out their sword. The term apparently dates from one
of the occupations of France by the Germans in the nine-
teenth century. Invading troops found themselves in the
Champagne region and seem to have put their cavalry
sabers to good use when liberating the contents of various cellars.

Coca: The manufacturers of Coca-Cola apparently pride
themselves that their product is the only one on the planet
that has two world famous names for it, namely Coca-
Cola and Coke. In fact, they have reason to feel even more
proud because the common word for their product in
France is neither Coca-Cola nor Coke but simply "Coca."
Going into a French bar and ordering *un Coke* will generally result in the barman repeating the order but with the
words *un Coca*. Ordering *un Coca,* provided of course that
you want one, is a good way of showing that you are starting to get the hang of things.

Coup: This word ostensibly means "a blow" or "a knock,"
which explains why, when someone offered me one in a bar
for the first time, I took a quick step backward. In fact *un
coup à boire* is a drink. When you suggest going out to a bar
with someone for a drink you might say, *"Je t'offre un coup*

à boire?" or possibly, *"Je te paie un coup?"* which is somewhat less chic. (As a general rule, when treating someone
to something, it is preferable to use *offrir* rather than *payer*.)
Encouraging someone to come for a drink might involve
saying, *"Allez! On va boire un coup?"* and heading off pur-
posefully toward the bar. As far as I can tell, *un coup* only
applies to alcoholic drinks: offering someone a soft drink
would be phrased differently, by saying, for example, *"Tu
veux boire quelque chose?"* You can specify that the drink
in question is red or white wine simply by adding the appropriate color. A glass of red wine is *un coup de rouge* but
calling it that does not say much for the quality of wine on
offer. Finally, if you overdo your consumption of *coups* you
are said to have *bu un coup en trop* or more colorfully *avoir
un coup dans le nez*.

DEUX . . . DEUX: If you listen carefully the next time you
go to a café or a brasserie, you will hear the double coffee
order. Assuming it is not the sort of place where the waiter
himself goes and makes the coffee, he will call the coffee
order to the barman, who will then get it ready and set the
cups ready on the bar. What is interesting is that the waiter
generally repeats the number of coffees ordered just after
the word *cafés*. Thus, instead of just shouting *"Deux cafés!"*
the waiter in fact cries, *"Deux cafés . . . deux!"* This is presumably intended to give the barman a second or so to jerk
himself from his reverie and think, "What? Did someone
call for coffee? But how many did he want?" whereupon
he hears the second *deux* right on cue. Some waiters do the

double order for any drinks, shouting orders like *"Trois Ricards . . . trois!"* This only seems to work for orders of a single sort of drink. Composite orders like *Deux pressions . . . deux, et un Ricard* sound silly.

EAU DE SOURCE: Knowing about this earlier would have saved us money. Arriving in France, one of the first things that you become aware of is the French obsession with mineral water. Plastic bottles of all shapes and sizes feature strongly on tables and desks across the land. At first sight, all the bottles have famous labels, Evian, Vittel, Volvic, and Contrex being the most popular. These actually all taste different, the easiest to spot being Contrex, which tastes more strongly of minerals than any of the others. Such branded mineral waters are, however, surprisingly expensive, even when bought in bulk. Then came the happy day when we discovered that a similar product exists at a fraction of the cost of the famous brands. This is generically labeled spring water or *eau de source* and it comes in plain, cheap, liter-and-a-half bottles, or can be bought even more cheaply in huge plastic containers that hold several liters. The only problem with these big containers is getting them home. But at least lifting them up to pour the water out is not a problem, as they have a handy tap on the bottom. There used to be (and perhaps there still is) a spot in Rue de la Pompe in Paris where spring water was freely available from a public tap. You would see people queuing with loads of empty mineral water bottles waiting to fill them up for free.

Pot: A drinks party at work to celebrate a wedding, a birth, or some happy domestic event is commonly known as *un pot*. People also do *un pot* on their last day at work before retiring or before leaving for a new job. When you learn that a colleague has handed in his notice, is about to get married, or has just had a baby, someone will invariably ask: *"Quand est-ce qu'il fait son pot?"*, sure in the knowledge that a *pot* will be organized. In the days preceding the *pot*, a collection will be held to buy a present, a procedure known as *faire passer une envelope*. You can, of course, have a *pot* at home, too.

Pourboire: The French word for "tip," which I include because any visitor to France should be aware that in French restaurants and bars, the tip is already included. In the old days, when you called for the bill, the waitress would add up all the things that you had ordered and then, in the blink of an eye, add on a fifteen percent service charge. Now the price of each thing shown on a menu already includes the tip. If you look at the bottom of a menu, it should say, in extremely small print, *"Service 15% inclus"* or some such. Hard as it may be to believe, I have seen menus in touristy restaurants where this phrase has been inadvertently mistranslated as "Service not included." How they came to make a mistake like that is beyond me! In bars, it is customary, if the barman or the waiter has been friendly, to leave a few centimes, despite the fact that you have really already tipped him. The only problem with the tip being included, and at fifteen percent it can be a sizeable sum, is that if the service or the food should be really awful, you can't really get out of paying it. In the old days, if things went badly, you would simply not have left a tip at all. It is not clear whether the enforced inclusion of the service charge has led to better or worse service in restaurants and bars.

ZINC: *Zinc* can be used to refer to a bar or to an aircraft, either of which meaning may come in handy. In either sense, it should be pronounced more like *zaing* than "zinc." Before the bars of French bistros came to be covered in tiles, synthetic materials, or imitation marble, the counter was made out of a sheet of zinc metal. Over the years, the metal surface became scratched and battered, giving the top of the bar a wonderful silvery patina. People would describe having had a drink *sur le zinc* rather than *au comptoir*, an expression which is still common, even though zinc-topped bars no longer are.

Bread *and* Cakes

AVEC CECI? This is the cry of bakers, greengrocers, and butchers as well as of any stall holder in a French market. You ask for your BAGUETTE, or a dozen merguez, or a kilo of potatoes and the seller, once he has handed you your order, nicely wrapped up, will then inquire, *"Et avec ceci?"* The question literally means "And with this . . . ?"

and is intended to check whether you need anything else. In the case where you have already asked for everything you really came in for, the question has a secondary, and more important, function. This is to inspire you to look at the various wares set out before you and spot something that you hadn't planned on buying when you came in and so increase the volume of the sale. Nine times out of ten you have no further purchase to make and thus will reply firmly, *"Ça sera tout, merci"*—that will be all, thanks. Oddly enough, while the salesperson will have greeted you, and possibly checked some aspect of your order, in a perfectly normal voice, the all important question *"Et avec ceci . . . ?"* will invariably be asked in a completely different, and generally irritating and ingratiating, tone. In my case, even though it may be kindly meant, the whiny, subservient tone of the question annoys me so much that I will reply, *"Ça sera tout, merci,"* whether I have actually thought of something else I need or not. Those unfamiliar with the question have been known to misunderstand it entirely, notably one local English resident who was asked the question each time he went to the butcher's. He thought he was being asked *"Et avec saucisses?"* and assumed that the butcher was enquiring whether he also wanted some sausages. His reply of *"Non merci, je n'en veux pas"* must have been perplexing to the poor chap.

BAGUETTE: Of course you know what this is, and so did I when I first arrived in France. What I didn't know was that you don't have to buy the whole thing. Buying a whole baguette, and then not eating all of it in the course of the day, used to annoy me intensely because the bread gets stale by the next morning. Until the day when I heard someone ask for *une demie baguette* at my local BOULANGE-RIE. Half a baguette was handed over without a raised eyebrow. Indeed, I now realize that quite a few people, especially single people, regularly only buy half. You can even buy two halves in the course of one day and thus enjoy fresh bread both for breakfast and in the evening. There is more: experts who particularly like a crusty or a less crusty baguette go on to request a baguette that is *bien cuite*—well done—or *pas trop cuite*—not too crusty. Another unexpected variant is offered by calling for something called *une baguette moulée*. This is a loaf that has been baked in a shaped baking tray, rather than on a flat plate, and thus has a lower half that is softer and less crusty. All this should enable you to broaden your bread-buying horizons enormously.

BOULANGERIE/PÂTISSERIE: Setting off to buy bread in France can lead you to being faced with a choice between two shops, both apparently selling bread, but one labeled *"Boulangerie"* while the other has a sign saying *"Pâtisserie."* What is the difference? And which one should you choose? *Une boulangerie* is a baker's shop. In it you should expect to find various sorts of bread, assorted PAINS AU CHOCOLAT, croissants and the like, collectively known as *viennoiseries*, and also a few nice cakes of assorted sizes and prices. These cakes will probably be in the shop window. *Une pâtisserie* is an upmarket version of *une boulangerie*. It will have a similar range of breads and *viennoiseries* but will have a far broader range of cakes of all shapes and sizes, all delicious, some of which will be very expensive indeed. If you just want bread, and are on a limited budget, it is probably a good idea to opt for *une boulangerie* so that you won't be tempted by the sight of all the amazing cakes in the *pâtis- serie*. This is especially good advice on the weekend when there are queues of people waiting for their cakes and tarts to be wrapped up. Some bakers who are particularly proud of their bread-making will label themselves as *boulangerie artisanale*. An *artisan* is a craftsman.

GÂTEAU: A word that has caused me great disappointment over the years. The problems arose because I learned it as being the French for "cake," a birthday cake, for exam- ple, being *un gâteau d'anniversaire*. The first time confu- sion arose was at a friend's house when, while making a cup of tea, we were asked, *"Vous voulez des gâteaux?"* Im- ages arose of chocolate cakes, or some delicious fruit affair stuffed with cream. I accepted enthusiastically, only to see my host return with a plate of plain tea biscuits. It seems that *gâteau* is a synonym for the French word *biscuit*, both words being used apparently interchangeably. If you are faced with an offer of a *gâteau*, the only way to know what you will get is by considering whether it's being offered in the plural: *des gâteaux*, or more specifically *des petits gâteaux*, in which case it is unlikely that there are several cakes on offer. Were really small cakes being considered, they would be referred to as *des pâtisseries* and not *des petits gâteaux*. Old-fashioned, hard English biscuits are generally called *des gâteaux secs*. Obviously, if something is being referred to as *sec*—dry—it is a good indication that rich chocolate cakes aren't being discussed. There are also salty nibbly things that are served with *un* APÉRO that are called *des gâteaux apéritifs* or *des gâteaux salés*. You really have to be on your guard whenever the word *gâteau* crops up in order to avoid being as disappointed as I was!

PAIN AU CHOCOLAT/CHOCOLATINE: This is an example of something whose name changes simply according to the area of France in which you order it. In Paris and in most of northern France, the delicious, flaky, buttery pastry roll with a length of chocolate inside it and which revives you, in time of need, at any hour of the day, is known as a *pain au chocolat*. If you head south, once you get below about the level of Bordeaux, and go into a local baker and call for a much needed *pain au chocolat*, you will be met with incomprehension. For in the south such things are called *chocolatines*. I find this to be such a novelty that, when on holiday, I have been known to rush into the first baker I see and order one merely for the joy of using the other word. Trying to order a *chocolatine* in northern France will, of course, be met by similar incomprehension. If you get completely lost on the way down to the south of France, and want to find out roughly where you are, ordering a *pain au chocolat* may be a useful way of finding out how far south you have actually gone.

TARTINE: The French have two words for bread-based snack foods. One is the word SANDWICH, and the other word is *tartine* which refers to a single piece of bread on which is laid or spread whatever it is that you are going to eat. *Tartines* do not necessarily have to have anything other than butter on them. Indeed, the ideal accompaniment to a cup of coffee in a bar early in the morning is *une tartine beurée* or two. This is a length of BAGUETTE cut lengthways and generously buttered. Dipped into your coffee, it becomes quite simply delicious. You can of course have *tartines* with jam or cheese should the fancy take you. If the bread you have is a bit stale, you can grill it and make a *tartine grillée*.

Food *and* Meals

À CHEVAL: The sight of an item on a brasserie menu called *hamburger avec oeuf à cheval* can lead to problems. In a country that is known for eating horses, the unwary may assume that the hamburger is made from horse meat. I have witnessed an English family in a café faced with such an item on a menu who, after several minutes of loud, dark muttering, were getting up to leave. I stopped them by pointing out that *à cheval* translates as "on horseback" and simply means that your hamburger is topped with a fried egg. Should a dish on a menu really contain horse meat—which is extremely unlikely—this would be specified as being *viande chevaline*. In the equally unlikely event that you actually want to buy horse meat, and shame on you if you do, you should go to a specialized butcher known as *une boucherie chevaline*. They are easy to spot, and to avoid, as they generally have a horse's head as a sign outside the shop.

BOUFFER: We will see in the final section that people do not work in France. You will be equally surprised to learn that a lot of them don't seem to eat, either. Rather than the word *manger*, many people use the familiar word *bouffer* when they talk about eating. Referring to consuming food as *bouffer*, however, makes it clear that what is being consumed is not expensive food of high quality—no one goes to La Tour d'Argent to *bouffer*! *Bouffer*, rather, refers to eating good, wholesome stuff in generous quantities. After a big meal, one might exclaim, *"C'est fou ce qu'on a bouffé!"* while the family is called to the table to eat by crying, *"À table—on bouffe!"* It is a good word to use if you are annoyed about someone eating all the chocolate: *"Qui a bouffé tout le chocolat?"*

There is a corresponding slang word for food itself, too, which is *la bouffe*.

CAFÉ GOURMAND: This is quite a recent idea, which you mainly come across in steak houses or fish restaurants that are part of a chain. You have enjoyed your *"entrée + plat"* but you don't really have enough room for a huge dessert, even though you quite fancy the idea of something sweet and preferably chocolatey. Realizing this, the restaurants came up with the brilliant idea of a *café gourmand*. The word *gourmand* doesn't relate to the coffee itself—it will just be the regular, small black espresso. The *gourmand* bit is what comes with the coffee. What arrives is an artistic array of a cup of coffee and a selection of miniature desserts. You generally get three: a mini triangle of brownie, an egg cup–size crème brûlée, and a taste of a fruit dessert like clafoutis. If you are having supper and don't want to be kept awake, you can always ask for a *déca gourmand*, where *déca* is short for *décaféiné*.

COUSCOUS, CASSOULET, CHOUCROUTE, CONFIT: In the course of the first few months that I spent in France I discovered several new culinary delights, all of which seemed to begin with the letter C. The first, and still my favourite, was couscous. As I'm sure you know, couscous is the name for ground semolina, a kind of beige granular powder to which you add a spicy vegetable sauce and some form of meat. It comes originally from North Africa; its widespread presence in France is due to the old French empire, which included the Maghreb (see Geography). The meat is generally lamb, whether in the form of chops or kebabs, chicken, or spicy sausages called *merguez*. You serve the ground semolina first, making a pile in the middle of your plate or bowl. Then you scoop on a good quantity of the vegetables, which include carrots, zucchini, celery, and parsnips together with a greater or lesser quantity of sauce depending on whether you like your dish dry or, as in my case, awash. You then place your chosen bits of meat on the top and you are ready.

After discovering couscous I went on to encounter *cassoulet*, which is a far heavier affair. It comes originally from either Toulouse or Castelnaudary in the southwest of France, depending on which cookbook you believe, and is a solid dish based on white beans cooked in a tomato sauce mixed with chunks of meat and sausage. It is great on winter evenings but is not recommended for those watching their waistlines.

Then you come to *choucroute*, which comes typically from the Alsace region in eastern France. *Choucroute* is based on pickled cabbage, cooked in white wine—which is far nicer than you might imagine—and is served with boiled potatoes, chunks of pork, sausages, slices of ham, and loads of mustard. You really have to wash it down with loads of beer, but you can drink white wine, too, if you prefer.

The final C that I encountered was *confit. Confit de canard* is a gastronomic delight. Chunks of cooked duck are preserved in a jar or a tin in large quantities of duck fat. You serve it by heating up the duck—whether on the grill or in the oven—and frying potatoes in the fat, and then you wash the whole lot down with a red wine such as Madiran from the southwest. This is quite simply paradise!

CRÈME ANGLAISE: I put this in because it contains the word *anglaise* and so, after spotting it on a menu, I was first inspired to order it simply out of patriotism. And I ended up quite glad I did! In simple terms, *crème anglaise* means "custard," but calling it that simply doesn't do it justice. It is custard revised and corrected. It is custard as it should truly be, or custard as it would have been if some country other than England had invented it. Come to think of it, that is just what the French did. *Crème anglaise* is more liquid, tastes more of vanilla, and is simply smoother and more sophisticated than custard, especially when the custard is made from powder out of a tin (even though I used to really enjoy mixing up the paste when I was smaller). All sorts of delicious French desserts, including such wonders as *gâteau au chocolat amer*, come with a serving of *crème anglaise*. Not only does it taste delicious, but you can have great fun spooning it all over your dessert and watching it run down the sides in an interesting way.

CUISSON: You have just ordered a hearty steak in a restaurant but, before the waiter sets off from your table, he will inquire, *"Et la cuisson?"* So, how do you want it cooked? There are four basic degrees of cooking that you can ask for. The first is *bleu*, or "blue." It theoretically means that the meat has been seared briefly on both sides while leaving the inside warm but not cooked through. It may well be called *bleu* because the meat is blue with cold since it certainly won't have been cooked much. Seeing *un steak bleu* for the first time, you may get the impression that it has only been shown to the cook before being brought to your table. It is an acquired taste, much like steak tartare. The next step up is *saignant*—"bloody." This corresponds to rare and means that the meat has actually been cooked rather than just left beside the stove. Purists believe that the best way to enjoy steaks is *saignant*. If that's what they like, fine. Then we come to *à point*, which is medium rare. This is considered a normal degree of cooking by many people, including most tourists. Things get tricky if you want to have your steak well done. You have two choices: either you go to a tourist restaurant where they don't care what you make them do to a steak, or you go to a normal restaurant and boldly ask for your steak *bien cuit*. If it is a steak restaurant, there is a fair chance that you are going to have to fight at this point. The waiter, proud in his role of self-appointed steak expert, will not take kindly to someone asking for a steak that he considers to be overdone. I have heard steak house waiters tell customers that if they want their steak *bien cuit* they can go and eat it somewhere else. If you don't feel up to a fight, you can take the easy option and order your steak *à point* and then drink lots of wine before it arrives. This cooking inquisition can also apply to other cuts of meat, for example *magret de canard*.

EAU: When ordering food in a restaurant, there comes a tricky moment when the waiter starts quizzing you about your water requirements. He will typically start off by casually suggesting that you might like some water, and you may well agree that this would be a good idea. Then, if you don't beat him to it, he will ask something like, *"Eau plate ou gazeuse?"* At this point, it is not too late to choose not simply between still and fizzy water but between those two and a jug of free tap water. All French restaurants are prepared to serve you with a jug of water should you ask for one. They would, of course, much rather sell you a nice bottle of mineral water. And if mineral water is what you generally drink, then why not? If you want a particular brand name, for example Vittel, then you can just order *une Vittel* rather than the more long-winded *une bouteille de Vittel*. What's more, if you are thirsty, but don't want to get too drunk too quickly, you can call for a bottle of mineral water as an APÉRO. You should however be warned that the more expensive the restaurant, the smaller the bottle of mineral water, and, inversely, the larger the bill. If you don't want to invest in mineral water, you should act quickly before anyone even starts mentioning it by calling for *une carafe d'eau*. Don't worry, even if you have been beaten to it by the waiter, you can still firmly request one at a later stage, though you may find yourself having to insist a bit.

FORMULE: This is a term featured on many menus, even those in restaurants not intended for tourists. *Une formule* is a fixed-price menu and can be expressed in a number of ways. *Formules* can be defined by price—*"Notre formule à 15 euro"*—or by name—*"Notre formule Rapide"* or *"Notre formule Pécheur"*—or simply by defining the elements that make it up. In this last case, *la formule* will specify whether it relates to three courses—*entrée, plat, dessert*—or to a choice between either *"entrée + plat"* or *"plat + dessert."* When you are strolling past a number of restaurants reading the menus that are displayed outside, it is very easy to misread a *formule* and believe that you are going to get three courses, only to find out once you are sitting down inside that it's only a choice of two. Touristy restaurants tend to advertise for the sort of customers they are seeking by offering a *formule touristique*. This is something that could well make you carry on to the next restaurant.

GALETTE: It is not so much the word *galette* that causes problems: rather, it is the ritual when such things are consumed that takes a bit of getting used to. A *galette* or, more precisely, *une galette des rois* is a round, flat, kind of covered sweet tart that contains a layer of marzipan. It has nothing to do with the biscuits called *galettes bretonnes*. A *galette des rois* is served, preferably warm, on Twelfth Night, January sixth, to celebrate the visit of the three kings to see the infant Jesus. A typical *galette* contains *une fève* or small ceramic figure of the baby Jesus. Whoever gets the *fève* in his or her slice of *galette* becomes king and has to wear the golden cardboard crown that is generally included with the *galette* by the baker. As you can sometimes spot the *fève* once the *galette* has been cut into slices, the French have developed an extraordinary ritual for sharing out the slices without any possible cheating. This ritual is followed both at home and, as I discovered to my astonishment, at work. A volunteer, often the youngest person available, is nominated by all those present and is expected to get down under the table in the room where the *galette* is being eaten. As each slice is put on a plate ready to be handed out, the person under the table is asked to name the person who should receive it. This is done for each slice to be served, the person under the table awarding himself with a slice at some point during the ceremony. The oddest thing about this procedure is the fact that no one appears to find it odd at all, even when it is carried out in an office!

LA CHANDELEUR: There are two traditional days on which the French eat crèpes. First of all, they are eaten as they are in England on Shrove Tuesday or Mardi Gras. But there is a second, particularly French, day for crèpe consumption known as *La Chandeleur*. This falls on February second and is a Christian feast day that corresponds to Candelmas, the day of Christ's presentation at the temple. Mind you, hardly any French people know what *La Chandeleur* signifies other than being an excuse for excessive consumption of crèpes. Apparently, it has something to do with the coming of the end of winter and the return of the sunlight. Not only are crèpes eaten on twice as many occasions in France as they are elsewhere, but the way in which they are eaten is different, too. As a boy in England, I was brought up to eat crèpes (on Shrove Tuesday but on no other date) with a squirt of lemon juice on them. Such an idea would never catch on with the sweet-toothed French. Here crèpes are eaten with granulated sugar sprinkled over them, preferably with a bit of fresh butter spread over them first. It beats lemon juice any day!

MANGER CHAUD: Food is important in France. The average French person will expect to eat meat at least once a day and will also expect at least one dish of each main meal to be served hot. Suggesting that a colleague might skip a decent meal and just grab a sandwich may well be met with an appalled cry of *"Mais, il faut manger chaud!"* or possibly *"Il faut manger chaud le midi"*—see MIDI. *Manger chaud* is not exactly grammatically correct—*chaud* is, after all, an adjective, not an adverb. Nevertheless, eating a hot dish at mealtimes is really sacred. We once stopped to buy wine at a vineyard in the wilds of France but hadn't realized that it was lunchtime. The lady of the house opened the door and promptly sent us packing complaining that we had disturbed them at the most inconvenient of moments, as *"On en est au chaud!"*—"We are at the hot course!" It wasn't only that we had shown great insensitivity by dragging her from her cooked meal. What really upset the woman was that we were ringing doorbells at a time when we should have quite obviously been having our own hot meal somewhere.

MARRONS: *Marrons* are chestnuts, a food that seems to feature quite prominently in the French diet. No Christmas meal—see RÉVEILLON—would be complete without a dish of chestnuts, though I for one have never managed to show much enthusiasm for cooked chestnuts at mealtimes. *Crème de marrons*, on the other hand, is a delicious, sickly sweet substance which is absolutely wonderful when stirred into *fromage blanc*. Wild chestnuts are known as *châtaignes*. A French tradition in the autumn involves going and picking up *châtaignes* in the forest and then roasting them over a log fire. Oddly enough, both *marron* and *châtaigne* are slang words for a punch. In rugby matches, when the players get upset about something and start thumping each other, the commentator may describe the generous exchange of punches as *une distribution de marrons.*

MONSIEUR: Clearly, this is not a food word, but it is a word that is often misused by foreign travelers in restaurants. On pleasant occasions when we have been out to eat with visiting friends, I have noticed that they can get carried away and become overly polite to the waiters. The problem stems from the fact that people tend to repeat what they hear. The waiter, addressing a male customer will politely call him *"Monsieur."* This is a quite right and proper thing for a well brought up waiter to do. Inexperienced foreign customers, however, try too hard to enter into the spirit of the thing and reply to the waiter by calling him *"Monsieur"* as well. This is silly. There is a kind of master-servant relationship between the two parties. While the waiter has to be subservient to the master, the master can't adopt the same deference in reply or the relationship breaks down. By all means, be polite to the waiter, but don't call him *"Monsieur"* when ordering. If you really want to, you can call him *"Monsieur!"* when trying to attract his attention. Some people do this, though most seem to just call, *"S'il vous plaît?!"* in an interrogative way. Incidentally, no one seems to call café waiters *"Garçon!"* anymore, even though 1950s French films encourage you to believe that you should.

PAIN: Bread at mealtimes is sacred in France. You only have to catch an evening commuter train to see loads of weary people clutching their BAGUETTES to eat with their supper. This means that in almost all French restaurants— we will come to the exceptions in a moment—bread will be given free, and without you having to ask for it. After visiting a few restaurants, you will realize that both the containers and the type of bread offered vary with the quality of the restaurant. The bread can come in a cheap, shiny metal basket, with or without a lining of paper napkin, or, if you move upmarket, it will be served in a rustic wicker basket with a pretty linen lining. The basic restaurant just provides diagonally sliced chunks of BAGUETTE. Spending more on your meal means that you can expect a selection of breads, both white and brown and even including the delicious sourdough-style bread known as *poilâne*. And what about butter? As far as I can see, you can only expect to be given butter in the most expensive places. But wherever you go, if you finish the bread you have been given, you can always ask for more. The only places where you don't seem to get bread are Asian restaurants and créperies.

PÈCHE: I am sure that the French fondness for things gas-tronomic explains why so many fruit and vegetable words are so commonly used to mean other things. For example, the word *pèche* means "peach" but *avoir la pèche* means to feel in really great shape. After your second cup of coffee at work, you might be heard to declare, *"J'ai vraiment la pèche* *ce matin!"* Another expression for this is *avoir la frite* where *frites* generally mean "french fries." *Poire* means "pear" but can also be a slang word for "face" or can be used in an expression *bonne poire* to mean "idiot" or "sucker." People tend to call themselves *bonne poire* after they have been forced into doing something unpleasant by someone with a strong personality. *Pomme*, meaning "apple," can also form part of an expression *pauvre pomme*, which also means "idiot" or "sucker." *Banane* is also a children's insult for an idiot. When it comes to vegetables, *patate*, which is a familiar word for "potato," can, like most of the preceding words, be used to mean "idiot." You hear children calling to each other, *"Eh! Patate!"*

SANDWICHS: The first thing to note is that the French plural of *sandwich* is *sandwichs*. The second thing is that when you order a *sandwich*, you get exactly what you ask for. You can easily check this just by ordering a ham sandwich in a bar. If you ask for *un sandwich au jambon* you will get one, but there won't be any butter on the bread because you haven't asked for any. If you want ham and butter in your sandwich, you have to ask for *un jambon beurre.* Doing this will mark you out as someone who knows about *sandwichs*, rather than some gormless person who stumblingly calls for *un sandwich au jambon avec du beurre*. If you want a ham and cheese sandwich, you should ask for *un mixte* or *un jambon fromage* but, again, there won't be any butter. And if you fancy *saucisson sec*, then just ask for that. However, if you want to be cool and get butter too you could order *un sec beurre*, which will get you both *saucisson* and butter for a minimum of effort.

TROU NORMAND: This is a wonderful thing that can transform a heavy meal, leaving a feeling of well-being where there might otherwise have been indigestion. In certain restaurants (generally the more expensive ones), when you are in the middle of a long and extravagant meal, the waiter will arrive unexpectedly with a small glass or dish containing a refreshing mix of sorbet and alcohol. This is a *trou Normand* and generally includes apple or lemon sorbet swimming in a generous shot of Calvados. It doesn't always feature on the menu but just appears at exactly the moment you are ready for it. Somehow, the mix of tangy sorbet and strong alcohol revives you from your food-and-drink-induced stupor and sets you up for the following courses. Other regions have variants on the theme using different flavors of sorbet mixed with the local brandy or marc.

The Country, and How to Get About It

Those who travel the country of France by car will learn how to avoid speeding fines and accidents and will also discover tempting reasons to drive around the Arc de Triomphe in the company of nervous passengers. Visitors planning to tour Paris on public transport will find that there are cheap tickets available, and everyone will discover the best phrase to shout when having your photo taken. And if you just want to wander around Paris on foot, you may pick up tips about where not to cross the road.

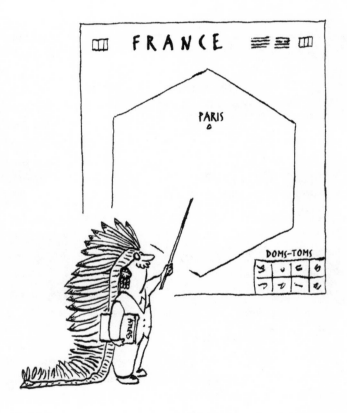

On *the* Road

APPEL DE PHARES: *Faire un appel de phares* is to flash your headlights at someone. In the U.K. and in the States, you flash your lights if you are in a good mood and want to let someone out from a side road, or allow an oncoming driver to turn in front of you. You can also do it aggressively to show how cross you are about something, often imagining that your lights are high-intensity lasers that will vaporize the offender and really teach him a lesson. While the French can flash their lights aggressively with the best of them, they are not used to lights being flashed kindly and rarely understand that you are signaling to let them out (probably because the idea of letting someone out has never occurred to them). However, the major use of flashed headlights in France is to warn someone coming the other way that he is approaching a police speed camera. Any driver worth his salt, if he spots a police car lurking by the roadside, or sees a radar trap, will flash the next two or three cars coming toward him to warn them of the impending danger. This shouldn't be seen as French generosity for the oncoming driver. Rather, it is simply a means of spoiling things for the policemen who are hiding in wait. So, if you are driving along a main road in France and two or three consecutive cars flash their lights, slow down! By the way, flashing your lights to warn other drivers is actually illegal in France.

BISON FUTÉ: This means literally "cunning bison" and tends to conjure up images of a particularly astute American Indian brave. The name was chosen by the French national road traffic organization, the people whose job it is to keep drivers informed of road work and advise travelers which days and times should be avoided when leaving or returning from holidays so to lessen the congestion around the major cities. *Bison Futé* publishes handy maps of secondary routes—known as *Itinéraires bis*—that they recommend, for example, if you want to try to avoid a six-hour traffic jam north of Lyons. These routes are indicated by road signs with green arrows and *"Itinéraire bis"* on them. *Bison Futé* also gives news bulletins on the television before particularly busy weekends advising drivers that the following Saturday will be a *journée rouge,* when driving should be avoided if at all possible. The only thing worse than a *journée rouge* is a *journée noire*, which generally occurs only on the weekend of the French public holiday in August when every car in France seems to be on the roads. People take *Bison Futé*'s advice quite seriously and can be heard refusing invitations for a weekend in the country because *"Bison Futé prévoit une journée rouge."*

CIRCULEZ!: This is the traditional cry of a French traffic policeman to a motorist and is quite mystifying when you first hear it. Despite what you might imagine, there is no intention involved to make anyone drive in circles. It is related to the word *circulation* which means "traffic flow" where no rotation is involved, either. When used by a policeman, the word *circulez* is just an instruction to keep on going, or, if you are stationary, to start moving as soon as possible. If you have been stopped for some reason by a patrolman, you will most likely be dismissed at the end of the interview with a brisk *"Circulez!"* or, if you have irritated him, by a distinctly sharper *"Allez! Circulez!"* It is generally a good idea to get going as soon as possible at this point. People, whether on foot or in a car, who have stopped to gawp at an accident or other roadside drama will be urged to stop staring and move on with the words *"Circulez! Il n'y a rien à voir!"*—"Move along! There's nothing to see!"

CLOUS: The correct term for a pedestrian crossing is *un passage clouté* but everyone seems to just call it *les clous*. In the U.K., a pedestrian crossing is intended to provide a safe place for a pedestrian to cross the road and is clearly marked with broad white stripes and silver studs so that motorists know that when they see a pedestrian waiting to cross the road, they should stop and let him or her across. The grateful pedestrian will thank the motorist and it is all wonderfully civilized and safe. Parisian pedestrian crossings look disconcertingly like British ones. They have the same broad white stripes and lines of silver studs, called *clous*, or "nails," clearly marking them. At first sight, therefore, they look deceptively inviting. However, the principal difference between the two nations' crossings is that, in France, the *clous* and the stripes do not define a safe place to cross; they define a target zone. In the unlikely event that a motorist spots someone waiting to cross at a crossing, he will feel more entitled than ever to try to run them over. In its way, it is all very civilized. Both Parisian motorists and pedestrians know that, if you want to cross the road, you do it elsewhere than at a crossing. By choosing a spot picked at random, far away from a crossing, the pedestrian will considerably increase his chances of survival. This means that if you ever happen to spot a tourist trying to cross the Champs Elysées at a crossing (and the mere fact that he is embarked on such a foolhardy attempt clearly marks him as a tourist), and you actually see a car stop and let him across, your first reaction should be to check the car's license plate number. I can guarantee that it will be foreign.

CONSTAT: The French like forms for things. A good example is a *constat à l'amiable* which is a jointly agreed accident report. This is a multicolored form that can be found in the glove box of practically all French cars. In the event of an accident, the two parties (assuming that there are two) pull themselves from the wreckage, shout at each other for a while, and then the calmer of the two will open his glove box and get out his *constat*. The form has two columns setting out, in the manner of a multiple choice questionnaire, various possible circumstances to describe what each party was doing at the time of the accident (for example, pulling out without looking, backing out onto a busy main road, or changing lanes to avoid a goat). Each party completes his column, adds a little drawing showing damage to each vehicle, and then each retains a copy to send to the insurance company. It is common to fill in the various details of the car make and registration number, as well as the insurance policy details, before putting the form in the glove box. (Well, I do.) This is intended to make completing the form in the event of an accident just a little bit easier. Interestingly, the French are amazed that in Britain we manage to have accidents and claim on the insurance without the benefit of a form like the *constat*. I have never been able to explain to their satisfaction how we manage to do so.

MPG: Visitors to France not only have to learn a huge number of new words, they also have to learn new ways of looking at common problems. In the U.S. and the U.K., the gasoline consumption of a car is measured in miles per gallon. This is an easy term to visualize as the bigger the number, the more efficient your car and the less gas you have to buy. France uses liters instead of gallons and kilometers instead of miles, and one might reasonably assume that gas consumption be measured in kilometers per liter. Not a bit of it. For reasons that I have never discovered, in France your car's efficiency is measured in l/100 km or the number of liters it will use to go 100 kilometers. Thus, the smaller the number of liters—eight or so—the better the consumption. In the U.K. and the U.S., it is a relatively easy matter when you fill up at a gas station to divide the number of miles you have driven by the number of gallons you bought and so get an idea of your mpg. In France, if you buy 44 liters of gas after driving 625 kilometres, it requires considerable mental agility to work out your l/100 km figures. I'll leave you to find the answer to this example.

PRIORITÉ À DROITE: One of the reasons driving in France is so memorable stems from the extraordinary French motoring rule known as *priorité à droite*. This is a simple rule that says that, unless there is an indication to the contrary, where two roads of any size intersect, the vehicle arriving from the right has priority over the vehicle on the other road. At first glance this seems simple. In fact it is quite simply mad. The rule means that if you are driving along any size road, a person on a little side road coming in from the right can, unless there is a sign to the contrary, just drive straight out in front of you, causing you to slam on your brakes in panic. If you are a careful sort and want to avoid sudden braking, you will tend to slow down, or even brake, at the first sight of a road joining from the right. You thus waste time and an incalculable amount of gas, for absolutely nothing. *Priorité à droite* is also very important at roundabouts (see ROND POINT). You even hear tales of people who are driving slowly along a quiet road whereupon a car leaps out from a hidden road to the right and causes a crash, but where the decrepit state of the merging car suggests strongly that the accident had been caused on purpose to claim the insurance of the person driving on the main road.

PV: PV is short for *un process-verbal* which, in its formal sense, means a written document intended to provide legally acceptable proof that an event of any nature took place. It can also mean the minutes of a formal meeting. In its more common form, however, it means a ticket, whether one given for speeding or for a parking offense. When complaining about being given one, no one ever says, *"J'ai eu un process-verbal"*—they call it *un PV*. Once you have landed yourself with a *PV*, you have two possible courses of action: if you are just a normal person with no connections, you just grumble and pay up. If, however, you have friends or relatives who work in government or in the police force, you take full advantage of this by asking whoever it is to simply make your PV disappear. This activity, which appears infuriatingly unfair to those of us who don't know anyone useful at all, is known as *faire sauter ses PV*. There is a rare third alternative that arises every five years at election time. Traditionally, the newly elected president will thank the electorate by declaring an amnesty of all outstanding parking fines and those traffic tickets that aren't considered too outrageous. I know colleagues who ignore final demands for payment in the months preceding an election in the hope of such an amnesty. You need nerves of steel!

ROND POINT: Roundabouts all used to be based on the PRI-ORITÉ À DROITE principle. Note this "used to be"; it is important. This principle meant that the person joining the roundabout had priority over the person already on it. You could therefore hurtle on to any roundabout with impunity, only to have to give way at the next road coming in. The rule was illogical and many roundabouts in France have since been changed so that the person already on the roundabout has priority over the one joining it. It is not clear, however, until you are very close to a roundabout in France and see the dotted white lines whether it is the old sort or the new sort. Indeed, many people still drive the old way regardless of the true nature of the roundabout. It is, of course, much more fun that way. The old rule still applies in many places, most notably at L'ÉTOILE in Paris, the roundabout around the Arc de Triomphe. This is a place where lunacy and anarchy apparently reign unchecked, but which in fact works on very clear principles. It is thus a great place to take visitors. They will be appalled by the apparent unchecked lunacy but will not necessarily have time to spot the underlying rules, mainly because they will be spending much of the time with their eyes shut or hiding under the seat. There are twelve streets joining L'ÉTOILE, one every thirty degrees or so. What makes the whole thing so special is that you have priority coming on to the roundabout but you lose it just as soon as the next road comes in from your right. If the traffic lights approaching L'ÉTOILE cooperate in your favor, you can absolutely hurtle into a maelstrom of moving cars with the happy knowledge that everyone will have to slam on their brakes to keep out of your way. Of course, the feeling of freedom is short-lived as you will have to slam on your own brakes shortly afterward in order to let in people from the next avenue. This is a good thing because it gives you a perfect excuse to do a good bit of tooting, alarming your already frightened passengers still further.

Public *Transport*

CARNET: On my first visit to Paris many, many years ago, I resolutely bought Métro tickets one by one as and when I needed them. It seemed perfectly reasonable to do so—it's what you do in London. This was unfortunate as, being an impoverished student who was trying to see as much of Paris as possible on the cheap, I would have been delighted to learn that there is a more economical way to buy them. Bought singly, a Métro ticket currently costs 1.40 euros. However, if you buy them in a group of ten, called *un carnet*, you only pay 10.70 euros. This works out at a considerable saving. *Carnet* literally means a "notebook or book." When you buy *un carnet de timbres* you actually get your ten stamps in a little book. However, when you order *un carnet* of Métro tickets you don't get a book, just ten individual tickets in a wad. RER tickets as well as suburban train tickets can also be bought more cheaply in *carnets*.

CARTE ORANGE: Travel cards for Parisian commuters are known as *cartes oranges*. As the name suggests, they are orange cards with the user's details and photo on them, wrapped in a plastic sleeve. The sleeve has a little pocket in it to hold the *coupon*, a plastic ticket the size of a Métro ticket that gives unlimited travel in a certain geographical zone of Paris for one month. Each month, people with a *carte orange* go to a Métro station and order *un coupon mensuel deux zones*, for example, and thus acquire another month's travel. Zones one and two cover central Paris, with zones three to six extending out into the suburbs. The cost of a *carte orange* is surprisingly reasonable. What's more, most employers reimburse half the cost of the *coupon* each month. There is now also a yearly travel card called Navigo, which works in the same way for a given geographical zone. This is slightly cheaper than a year's worth of monthly *coupons* and also avoids you having to go and stand in line at the ticket office each month. Its other main advantage is that you just have to wave it over the ticket barrier rather than stopping to take out your *coupon* and pass it through a reader.

COMPOSTER: Much confusion arose the first time I saw signs at a railway station instructing me to *composter* something or other. In fact, it has nothing to do with gardening; *composter* means to punch your train ticket. At the end of each platform in any railway station in France you will find one or more orange pillars of about four feet height. You simply slide the end of your ticket into a slot near the top of the pillar and you are rewarded by a loud stamping sound. Retrieving your ticket will reveal it to have a semicircular hole punched along one edge and the date stamped at one end. You may be tempted not to *composter* your ticket in the hope of using it another time. This is not a good idea at all as ticket checks by *controlleurs* are frequent and it is less likely nowadays that you can escape a fine by simply pretending to be a stupid foreign tourist. (Please excuse the tautology.) Before resorting to increased fines, the railway company tried to discourage people from catching trains without a ticket by having a poster campaign based on the slogan *"Frauder, c'est bête"*—"Fare dodging is stupid." This was withdrawn quite rapidly because most of the posters were defaced with the additional words *"Mais payer, c'est encore plus bête"*—"Paying is even more stupid."

RATP, RER, SNCF: Commuter travel in Paris is handled by three different mass transit companies. The Métro lines and all the Parisian buses are the responsibility of the RATP—La Régie Autonome des Transports Parisiens—which was created in 1949. The fact that one company handles both means of transport means that a Metro ticket can also be used to catch a bus. This is practical because you can keep a CARNET in your wallet so as to be free to use either means of transport as the need arises. Métro lines, like bus routes, are known by a number, while the direction on the Métro is shown by the name of the terminus. The RER—Le Réseau Express Régional— looks after the suburban lines that are each known by a letter rather than a number, and which sweep across Paris from north to south and from one side to the other. RER trains are much bigger than Métros, go faster, and often have two floors. In addition to suburban RER lines, there are also suburban railway lines leading to the main railway stations. These lines are run by the SNCF—*Société Nationale des Chemins de Fer*—which also runs the main long-distance trains. Unless you have a CARTE ORANGE, you will need separate tickets for the RER and SNCF trains outside central Paris.

Geography

DOM-TOM: When France gave up its empire after the Second World War, the word *colonie* was officially banned. What remains of the French empire is now known as *les DOMS-TOMS*. The letters stand respectively for *Départements d'Outre Mer*, or overseas counties, and *Territoires Outre Mer*, or overseas territories. The French *départements* or counties include four that are overseas, namely Guadeloupe, Martinique, Guyana, and Réunion. These are considered to be ordinary French counties, even though they are rather a long way from all the others. They are generally shown on the handy little map that you get at the back of French diaries or planners. The TOM are more independent and even farther away and comprise New Caledonia, French Polynesia Wallis-et-Futuna, St. Pierre-et-Miquelon, and the French Southern and Antarctic Lands.

CHARLES TIMONEY   43

HEXAGONE: If you look at a map of France on its own, half-close your eyes, and let your imagination loose, you might start to believe that the country is roughly hexagonal. If you ignore the fact that the coasts and inland borders are far from straight, such a notion is not that far-fetched. A first side of the hexagon begins at the bottom of the Atlantic coast, down by Spain, and stretches up to Brest. The second goes from Brest to the Belgian border. From there, the third side heads southeast down into Alsace. The fourth side links Alsace to Monaco, while the fifth goes over to the start of the Pyrenees. The final side goes from there back to St. Jean de Luz on the Atlantic coast. Having carried out this exercise in visualization, you may be wondering what the point of it all was. It was necessary in order to appreciate why the French refer to their country as *l'hexagone*. This is something that they do quite often on news and weather programs.

MAGHREB: The old French empire included the Maghreb. This is the collective name for Algeria, Morocco, and Tunisia. A native of any of these countries is commonly known as a *Maghrebin*. There is also a common term used for a native of Algeria, or, more precisely, from a particular mountainous region of Algeria, which is *Kabyle*.

Paris *and* the Suburbs

L'ÉTOILE: The Charles de Gaulle Airport, which is north
of Paris, and La Place Charles de Gaulle, home to the
Arc de Triomphe, have something in common: hardly
anyone, except tourists, who don't count, refers to them
by their proper name. No Parisian would dream of getting into a taxi, or buying an RER train ticket, and asking for *"l'aéroport Charles de Gaulle, s'il vous plaît."* People
just call the place *l'aéroport de Roissy* or, more commonly,
just Roissy, which is the name of the place where the airport was built. Thus, when asked where they are flying
from, people will reply, *"Je pars de Roissy."* Similarly, when
the area around the Arc de Triomphe is referred to, it is
just known as *L'Étoile*, taxi drivers asking, *"On passe par
l'étoile?"* while Métro passengers say things like *"Je vais de-
scendre à Étoile"* or *"il faut changer à Etoile."* Some people
try to compromise by calling it Place Charles de Gaulle-
Étoile, but this is impossibly long-winded. All this should
not lead you to believe that the late "Grand Charles" is
in any way unpopular. It is just that people find the old
names easier and quicker to say.

NEUF-TROIS (93): The counties or *départements* outside
Paris have numbers that go from 91 to 95, Paris itself being
75, as you may know. Each of these neighboring *departe-
ments* has a completely different social character, ranging
from les Hauts de Seine just to the west of Paris, which
is by far the most chic—I used to live there—through

l'Éssonne to the south and le Val de Marne to the east, neither of which is particularly remarkable. To the northeast, however, lies la Seine Saint Denis whose county number is 93. This should be pronounced *quatre-vingt-treize*, assuming that you are ever forced to talk about it. However, the residents of this department enjoy such an unfavorable reputation in the eyes of Parisians that people have taken to calling it *le neuf-trois* instead. This is intended to show, somewhat cruelly, that inhabitants of "93" are so dim that they can't even pronounce the complicated number of their own county and are forced to call it by the individual figures instead. Anyone who is lucky enough to live elsewhere will refer to *les habitants du neuf-trois,* making sure that they pronounce it in as unflattering a way as possible. People like to note the license plate of cars—the last two figures showing which county a car comes from—and, when they spot a 93 driving badly, exclaim loudly, *"Ça m'étonne pas—c'est un neuf-trois"*—"what do you expect from a 93?"

PARIGOT: The inhabitants of Paris, or those who were born there and still bear the hallmarks, are *Parisiens*. This is often replaced by the slang term *Parigot*, which can either refer to a person or be an adjective. A Parisian accent is thus *un accent parigot.* However, Parisians do not necessarily enjoy the best of reputations in the eyes of the inhabitants of the rest of France, being seen as aggressive, proud, and rude. What's more, the fact that French car number plates have the number of the county of origin as their last two figures means that they can easily be spotted when away from their home city. Poor Parisians driving throughout the rest of France when on holiday are regularly subjected to derisive cries from the locals of *"Eh! Parigot!"* When circumstances demand stronger criticism, as they often do, angry locals may shout unflattering things such as *"Parigot—tête de veau!"*

PÉRIPHÉRIQUE: Years ago, an original inner ring road was built in Paris and named *les Boulevards des Maréchaux* because each section of the ring is named after one of Napoléon's marshals. Today, these boulevards are just ordinary roads and thus are festooned with traffic lights and junctions, which make them almost unusable at rush hour. By the end of the 1960s it was clear that a new continuous ring road was necessary, and so the Boulevard Périphérique was constructed. This road is generally known as *le périphérique* or even *le périph* and it forms a thirty-kilometer-long circle around Paris. It is thought of as forming the geographical limit of the city: everything beyond it lies in a new county. The area within the ring is known as *Paris intra muros*, or Paris within the city walls, even though the walls are no longer standing. The ring has a series of exits that allow you to head into a given part of Paris or out into the suburbs. These are known as *portes*. Several *portes* form the beginning of highways out of the city. One of the first things to learn when navigating around Paris is the location and name of the principal *portes*. For if you don't know where the exit that you want lies, you may end up going the wrong way around the circle. The lanes of the *périphérique* aren't referred to as northbound or westbound, but rather as inner and outer lanes—*périphérique intérieur* and *périphérique extérieur*. You are supposed to realize that when you are on the inner lane, Paris is on your right as you go round and deduce your direction accordingly.

SEIZIÈME: Paris is divided into *arrondissements* or administrative districts. Prior to 1860, there were only twelve *arrondissements*, but when Haussmann was asked to redesign the city he grabbed eleven outlying villages and made them part of Paris. In case you are in any way interested, this increased the area of the city from 3,288 hectares to 7,088 hectares. Thus, since 1860 there have been twenty numbered *arrondissements* which are arranged in a clockwise spiral that starts with the 1er (*premier*) which is centered on the Louvre and ends with the 20ème (*vingtième*, or twentieth) on the far right hand or eastern side of the city. Each *arrondissement* has its own character—for example the 13ème is the Asian district while the 8ème has all the expensive shops. The *arrondissement* that seems to have the strongest character, or at least the most notable reputation is the 16ème or *seizième*, for the 16ème is where the rich people live. While you can find some hugely expensive houses, it is mostly made up of old-fashioned, well constructed apartment buildings with magnificent front doors and marble hallways. These are inhabited by rich, generally chic people who wear their fur coats to walk their little dogs in the Bois de Boulogne. Concierges, and even maids, can still be spotted in the 16ème. Seizième is thus, or possibly used to be thus, an adjective that means rich and chic.

Miscellaneous (*but* Necessary) Travel Words

OUISTITI!: Should you ever be asked by a French person to take their photo in front of some famous monument somewhere, there is no point in pointing their camera at them and saying brightly, "Say cheese!" For a start, if you stand in front of a mirror and say cheese with a silly French accent, it will not produce the photogenic rictus that you were hoping for. The main problem, however, is that a French tourist will not be expecting to be asked to say "cheese" because in France, when being photographed, people say "ouistiti!" Like "cheese," the success of the photograph depends on the accent used when saying the word. If you say *ouistiti*—it means "marmoset," by the way—in a flat English accent reminiscent of the cartoon dog Droopy, you will look thoroughly miserable on the photo. If, on the other hand, you say it enthusiastically in a strong French accent, the two last syllables force your mouth sideways into a broad grin. Just in case you are planning on asking a French person to take your photo one day, there is a slight chance than in place of *ouistiti* he may let his fondness for things culinary win through and ask you to say omelette!"

PERPÈTE: France seems to lack the really extraordinary place names that you seem to find in the U.K. such as Nether Silton, Appleton le Moors, or Claxeby Pluckacre. This perhaps explains why the French have devised some striking terms for places that they can't remember the real name of or for places that they can't be bothered to call by their proper names. If a Frenchman wants to refer to a place without using its proper name, and convey just how far away and off the beaten track such a place is, he will call it *Perpète les Oies*. If someone has bought a cottage lost in a small village miles and miles from Paris, this will be described as *"il a acheté une petite maison à Perpète les Oies."* *Perpète* means "miles away" while *les Oies*—"the geese"— shows how rural it is. If, on the other hand, you want to convey not so much how far away it is but just the fact that the place in question is somewhere or other, it doesn't really matter where, you would call the place *Triffoullis les Oies*. When telling someone that you had to go somewhere a fair way away in order to find what you were looking for, you would say, *"J'ai dû aller à Triffouillis les Oies pour le trouver."* *Triffouillis* probably comes from the verb *triffouiller*, which means "to rummage about."

A SIDE NOTE ON PLACE NAMES IN FRANCE: How many cities have their own adjectives that can be used to define their residents? Not that many. You can encounter people who define themselves as being Londoners, or Liverpudlians, or New Yorkers, or Bostonians. But people from Stoke on Trent or Morton in Marsh would be hard put to come up with an adjective to describe themselves simply by virtue of the town they live in. In France, things couldn't be more different: whatever town, village, or city you come from, there is an adjective ready and waiting to describe you. Dictionaries show lists of the principal ones, some of which you can guess, like *Parisien* for Paris and *Lyonnais* for Lyons. Others are far more obscure. The inhabitants of Bourges, a sizeable cathedral town in central France, are not called *Bourgeois*, as might be assumed. They are known as *Berruyers*. This is as hard to pronounce as it is to guess. Logic does not necessarily play a part in the selection process for these adjectives. When we used to live in Neuilly, we were *Neuilléens*. Inhabitants of Neuilly-Plaisance, which is somewhere else entirely, are called *Nocéens*. There are adjectives for the inhabitants of every single village, however small. Such adjectives may not be used much, especially when the village only has a couple hundred inhabitants, but they are there should they be needed.

These adjectives to define the residents of a particular town or city are used far more often in France than they are in other countries, and, as far as I can see, are mainly used to describe prominent sporting figures. In a newspaper article that describes the exploits of a sportsman in a recent event, the person will be referred to by his full name at the beginning of the article. Later references tend often to be made using the adjective relating to the city of his birth. For example, Jean Alesi, who comes from Avignon, was invariably referred to as *"l'Avignonnais"* in practically any article about him. As far as I know, no French female star hails from the town of Belcombe. This is probably a good thing, as women from Belcombe are unfortunately known as *Belcombaises*. This sounds remarkably like *belle qu'on baise* which means "beautiful woman who gets bonked." I am sure that the French habit of describing people by their city of origin is inextricably linked with their obsession with place of birth—see LIEU DE NAISSANCE in the "Paperwork" chapter.

VERGE: I have put this word in at the end, not because I believe that you necessarily need to know it before going to France—though this may depend on what sort of thing you do on your holidays—but rather so that you can appreciate why French people find a common English road sign particularly amusing. For *verge* is the proper French word for the male sexual organ. Thus, French people driving along English country roads when on holiday are much amused by signs that warn that the shoulder at the side of the road is unstable by proclaiming, "Soft verges."

ℰDUCATION

When on holiday in France you may find yourself talking to locals who, given the French fondness for boasting about their offspring's prowess, may well try to regale you with tales of their educational success. Higher and further education in France is surprisingly different from the systems in the U.K. and the U.S.: the exams are different, the marking system is different, and the grade reports are different. Even the reference books are different, as we will see.

What's more, for those who choose to take it, the road to higher education in France is longer and harder than it is in the U.K. and the U.S.

We will discover a handy French term for going back to school and marvel at the fact that one can call oneself an intellectual in France and no one will laugh.

School

BAC: *Le bac*, the familiar form of *le baccalauréat*, is a word that strikes terror into the hearts of both French school-children and their parents. *Le bac* is the name for the exam that you take at the end of your secondary education, and roughly corresponds to A levels in the British system. In my day in England, when you reached the sixth form at the tender age of fifteen or so, you were expected to select the three subjects that you were going to concentrate on for the next two years. The subjects I chose, and fairly rapidly regretted choosing, were math, physics, and chemistry. For two long years I studied nothing but these three subjects—apart from doing an English course to make sure I could at least read and write, plus a bit of sport now and again. In France things are quite different. At the age of fifteen you can select between three main types of *bac* known as Bac S, Bac ES, and Bac L, but whichever you choose you will be required to study a wide range of at least eight subjects. In addition to your principal subjects—math if you go for a Bac S (considered by many to be the elite among *bacs*); econom-ics and math if you opt for a Bac ES; and literature, should

you decide on a Bac L—you will also study and be marked
on other subjects including history, geography, two modern languages, sports (yes, there is a sports exam that counts
toward the final total), and even philosophy (see below).
There are written exams for all subjects except sports, as
well as oral exams for the modern languages. Marks are
attributed according to the most arcane of systems—see
COEFFICIENT—and are given out of twenty for each subject.
Then, a total mark is also calculated out of twenty based on
the individual mark for each subject. You need a score of
ten or higher to pass. The important thing is that you have
to do sufficiently well in your favorite subjects in order to
ensure that your weaker subjects don't bring down your average mark too much. Passing the exam—*avoir son bac*—is
enough for most people. However, getting marks that are
well above average will lead to various levels of distinction,
namely *assez bien, bien*, and *très bien*, known collectively as
bac avec mention. Any one of these looks good on a CV and
may help in later life.

COEFFICIENT: This is a tough one! In important exams in
France, notably le BAC but also in university exams, you
have the extraordinary situation where marks for different
subjects do not all count the same toward the total mark.
Each exam is weighted according to a scale that is usually expressed as a number between one and eight. When
a paper has been marked and the candidate has scored,
for example, twelve out of a possible twenty, the mark is
multiplied by the *coefficient*—often shortened to *coef*—to

give a final mark for that paper. Some subjects are heavily weighted, for example maths, while others like sports have a *coef* of one or two. This means that if your offspring is very good at lower-weighted subjects and not so good at math, he or she will be in trouble. Conversely, the happy few whose favorite subjects have the highest *coef* can generally relax and put their feet up when it comes to taking the other subjects. From the very first parent-teacher meeting at the start of the *baccalauréat* period, everyone is made aware of the various *coefficients* and thus spends the next two years worrying. The weightings of the various subjects vary enormously between the three main types of *baccalauréat*. This should definitely encourage you to select the one that best suits your child's talents in order to increase his or her chances of success.

PHILOSOPHIE: As we have just seen under BAC, whichever type of *baccalauréat* exam you choose to sit, it will include a philosophy paper. This is known as *l'épreuve de philosophie*, or more commonly as *l'épreuve de philo*. When I first heard of this I had the greatest difficulty in accepting the fact that children of all disciplines should be expected to sit a philosophy exam. Not only does everyone face it, whether they are specializing in math, literature, or economics, but the subject itself is one of national importance. For, in June when the BAC takes place, one of the major topics on the evening news on the day of the philosophy paper is taken (and everyone sits the exam on the same day) are the questions that were set that year. People take a real interest in the questions, mainly, I think, to comfort themselves that they wouldn't have been able to pass with a question like that. To show what schoolchildren are faced with, I set out a few questions from previous years' *philo* papers:

- *L'ennui est-il caractéristique de l'être humain, ou de certaines époques de l'histoire?*—Is boredom typical of human beings, or of certain periods in history?
- *L'idée de pauvreté se réduit-elle à une catégorie économique?*—Can the idea of poverty be reduced to an economic category?
- *Peut-on s'attendre à tout?*—Can anything happen?

LA RENTRÉE: This single word is one of the most typical of the French language. In its literal sense *la rentrée* corresponds to the notion of "going back to school," but it astonishes French people that we can manage without a proper single word for the thing like they have. In most houses, *la rentrée* is a term that strikes terror into everyone's hearts. In shops you see signs urging you to buy school supplies and children's clothes *pour la rentrée*. The children hate it because it means the end of the long summer holidays. The parents don't like it much because it means several trips to the shops to buy books, files, pens, and all the other essentials, which seem to have vanished since the end of the previous summer term. However, the concept of *la rentrée* is much broader than the simple return to school or university. *La rentrée* covers the whole post-holiday period, which generally spans the end of August and the first half of September, and there are even people for whom *la rentrée* extends well into October. For example, at work, if you are faced with something that you don't want to deal with in June, you can say *on verra ça à la rentrée*—we will deal with that after the holidays. The lack of precision in this example is an advantage to the person who is putting off whatever it is until as late a date as possible. At home the term is used as well for fixing future engagements. In the summer, your friends will probably go away for a large part of the summer, though not necessarily at the same time as you, and therefore it is possible that you won't see them from the end of June to the beginning of September. The last thing you will say to each other will be along the lines of *"Vous viendrez dîner à la rentrée"*—we'll see you for supper after the holidays. This shows that you want to see them, but aren't that keen to fix a date at this stage.

SÉCHER: If you know the verb *sécher* you probably know its principal meaning, which is "to dry" in the manner of towels or things that are left out in the sun. However, in the context of education, *sécher* takes on other meanings. For a start, if you feel when you get up in the morning that you really can't face going to school and decide to skive off (or play hooky, or whatever it was you said at your school) you would be said to *sécher les cours*. But the word also means to dry up metaphorically when you have no idea of how to reply to a teacher's question. Pupils are heard to exclaim despairingly, *"Je sèche"* when faced with a question they can't answer or to mutter darkly when asked how their day went, *"J'ai séché en math."* If they don't want to get stuck and find themselves thinking *"Je sèche"* during a test, they may decide to cheat and prepare what we used to call a crib sheet, a hidden piece of paper that has helpful notes written on it. Such hidden notes are known in French as an *anti-sèche*. This term can still be used in later life—colleagues who are getting ready for a tough meeting are heard to say, *"Je prepare mon anti-sèche."*

SOLEIL: Those of you who have ever been bored in tedious science lessons at school will know the pastime of typing long numbers into a calculator which, when the calculator is turned upside down, reveal a word. For those who never did this sort of thing, a calculator 4 looks like an h when upside down, 3, 5, 7, and 8 making respectively E, S, L, and B. The longest word we came up with was *Shelloil* which, while quite long, isn't all that funny. You won't be surprised to learn that French students while away boring lectures in just the same way. They come up with words like *soleil*—sun—but also with *elle bese*. *Elle bese* is a lot funnier than *shelloil* because it sounds like *elle baise*. *Elle baise*, as we will see under BAISER, means "she bonks."

TABLE DES MATIÈRES: In an English reference book, the contents page is right at the front. This is handy because you can open the book, look at the contents, and then carry on leafing through in the same direction until you reach the chapter that you are looking for. The French motto when it comes to reference books appears to be, "Why be logical?" because they put their *table des matières* at the back of the book. This means you have to open the book at the back, spot the chapter that you want, and then scramble back in the opposite direction searching for the chapter. The only possible explanation for putting the *table des matières* at the back is for French readers, having finished the book, to be able to scan through the list and think, "Oh yes! I enjoyed Chapters 7 and 12." The English, on the other hand, have the advantage of deciding right from the beginning which chapters they think they might enjoy.

TIRETS: There are two quick ways of telling whether a book is English or French (we shall suppose, for sake of argument, that you have become so perfectly bilingual that you no longer notice whether words are in French or English): The first is used when books are standing upright in a bookcase. If you have to tilt your head to the right to read the wording down the spine, the book is English; if you tilt your head to the left, it is French. Please spare me a thought as I sit here checking my bookcase to test the theory for you and getting a sore neck. Why French printers print their spines the wrong way round is unclear. It is certainly illogical because it makes checking across a bookshelf, from left to right, in search of a particular book very uncomfortable.

The second quick way to spot the origin of a book is to

open to a page and look at the conversations. An English book will say something like:

> *"Isn't this a brilliant description of things French?"*
> *Sarah exclaimed admiringly.*

Whereas in a French book, a line of speech begins with a dash instead of quotation marks. A spoken sentence will thus look like this:

> *—En effet, s'écria Sébastien, C'est vraiment génial!*

Conversations in novels thus begin with a dash, known as *un tiret*, a word I first learned when one of my wife's aunts confessed that she only read the bits of a novel that started with a *tiret*, saying proudly, *"Je ne lis que là où il y a des tirets."*

VINGT: As I've mentioned, one of the first things you have to learn about education—whether primary, secondary, or higher—in France, is that all marks for tests or exams are given out of a possible score of twenty. Even the results of LE BAC are given out of twenty. At school, each child has an ongoing average mark, based on tests, homework, and continuous assessment, which is always out of twenty. People tend to note and remember the marks their children get in the principal subjects and then, assuming that the marks are something they are proud of, and not, as equally often happens, completely ashamed of, they regale their friends and acquaintances with tales of little François's brilliance in, for example, math. It is common to see two or more women (for men don't seem to do this) sitting in a group in some form of public transport with one of the group doing her utmost to drive the others to distraction by telling them all the good marks that her marvelous offspring has achieved. For example, *"François a eu dix-huit en maths cette année!"*—François got eighteen out of twenty in math this year. Clearly, this activity is all the more rewarding for the speaker if she knows or suspects that her audience's children have not achieved the same dizzy heights of academic success. Indeed, the bigger the gulf between the respective children's marks, the more fun the game.

After *the* "Bac"

CLASSE PRÉPARATOIRE: In France, if you want to become an engineer, which means going to one of the GRANDES ÉCOLES, or if you are aiming for one of the elite schools of literature or business, you have to go to a *classe préparatoire*. This involves spending two years (or three if you fail the exams) in a special *lycée* immediately after passing your *baccalauréat*. Of course, no one calls it *classe préparatoire*; they just call it *prépa*. Thus, proud parents, in reply to your inquiry as to what their offspring are doing at the moment, will say things like, *"Il est en prépa au Lycée Louis-Le-Grand"*—Lycée Louis-Le-Grand in Paris being one of the better *lycées*. Your chances of passing the entrance exam and getting in to the best GRANDES ÉCOLES are, of course, considerably improved if you go to one of the top *lycées* to do your *prépa*. Indeed, in later life, people are more likely to name-drop about their *prépa* than about their ordinary *lycée*. *Classe préparatoire* being terribly elitist, there are all sorts of "in" terms for the course, or for redoing one of the years. For example, if you are preparing to do engineering, the first and second years of *prépa* may be known as *hypo-taupe* and *taupe*, respectively, while should you be hoping to study literature later on, your classes will be referred to as *khâgne* (pronounced "kyne") and *hypokhâgne*.

GADZART: If you only just come on holiday to France now and again you will very likely never hear this word. I only include it because it illustrates the cultlike side of French higher education. The French like to give insider names to the people who have attended their top universities. For example, the engineering school with one of the best reputations is l'École Nationale Supérieure d'Arts et Métiers, often just known as "Les Arts." "Gadzart"—a shortened form of *un gars des Arts* (where *gars* means "bloke")—is the name for one of its pupils. If you are lucky enough to be *un gadzart*, you can count on the support of other past pupils once you leave to give you preferential treatment when applying for a job, and to help you move upward once you have got it. You hear colleagues explaining someone's meteoric rise in a company by saying, *"C'est normal: c'est un gadzart."* Another famous term for pupils of a top university is *enarque*. This is someone who has attended the elite École Nationale d'Administration and who will probably end up a member of Parliament, or even prime minister. The ENA's ambitions are modestly summed up by its motto of *"la formation des décideurs publics de démain."*— training tomorrow's public deciders.

GRANDES ÉCOLES: In the U.S. and the U.K., if you want higher education, there is really nowhere better than one of the top universities. French universities are okay in their way, but a step above is one of the *Grandes Écoles*. *École* in this context doesn't mean "school" as in high school, but rather a place of education. *Grandes Écoles* specialize either in science—in which case they are known as *écoles d'ingénieurs*—business studies, or commerce. Famous *Grandes Écoles* include ENA—l'École Nationale d'Administration, HEC—Hautes Études Commerciales, and, of course, l'École Polytéchnique. If all goes well, you spend three years at a *Grande École*. However, in order to get in, you have to spend at least two years in a CLASSE PRÉPARATOIRE, which means that an engineering degree, for example, requires a grand total of five years' study in France.

MATHS SUP, MATHS SPÉ: We have seen that if you want to get into one the *Grandes Écoles*, you have to spend two years in a CLASSE PRÉPARATOIRE after taking your *baccalauréat*. If you are aiming to get into one of the elite engineering schools, your time spent at the CLASSE PRÉPARATOIRE will involve studying a huge amount of math. The first and second years of CLASSE PRÉPARATOIRE are respectively known as *mathématiques supérieures* and *mathématiques spécialisées* and are notoriously tough. Indeed, students work so hard that many barely see the light of day for two years. However, as usual, no one ever refers to these two years as *mathématiques supérieures* and *mathématiques spécialisées*. Proud parents, or the offspring themselves, invariably shorten the terms to *maths sup, maths spé*. Unfortunately, the first time (or even the second time) someone informs you that they are doing "matsoup matspay" there is no way on earth that you are going to understand that they are spending two horrendous years between school and university studying higher mathematics.

X: Imagine that you are going to see someone for the first time at a business meeting and you ask your colleague what the person is like. If they reply that *"Il a fait l'X"* or that he is *"X mines,"* will you be any the wiser? Even if you have heard of the most elite of all French engineering schools, the *nec plus ultra* of GRANDES ÉCOLES that is l'École Polytéchnique, will you make the connection? École Polytechnique is the foremost GRANDE ÉCOLE of engineering where pupils are as much soldiers as students. The entrance exam, which is taken after two years of CLASSE PRÉPARATOIRE, preferably at the best *lycée*, assuming you can get in, is the toughest of all. However, once you graduate, having survived a total of five years including the two in CLASSE PRÉPARATOIRE, the deference of your peers is assured and you are made for life. École Polytéchnique is generally known by the abbreviation "X." This comes from the emblem of the school which shows two cannons crossed in the shape of an X. The *mines* part refers to what a person has specialized in studying at "l'X,", as opposed, for example, to studying *ponts* or "bridges." Of these, *mines* or mining is without doubt the acme of French education. Being the product of the acme of French education, *X mines* have a very high opinion of themselves and a correspondingly low opinion of everyone else. I know several *X mines*, only two of whom I can count as friends.

And *Later*

INGÉNIEUR: When I started my job in Paris I discovered that I was referred to as *un ingénieur* because I had an engineering degree as well as my patent qualifications. While I understood what the word meant, I didn't realize how important it is in France. While the word just means "engineer," it has a whole spirit and history that the English word doesn't have. Where the word "engineer" is used fairly generously in English to cover both people who know something about engineering and people who have nothing whatsoever to do with it, its use in French is much more regulated. You don't find garbagemen in France being called "refuse engineers" and the bloke who comes to service our boiler would never claim to be a "heating engineer." To be called *un ingénieur* in France you have to have an engineering degree to back it up. Engineering degrees only come from *une école d'ingénieur* and preferably from one of the GRANDES ÉCOLES.

INTELLECTUEL: One of the amazing things about France is that a French person can seriously define himself as an intellectual without being thought of as pretentious or requiring any further sort of job description. When there is a panel of experts leading a discussion on the TV, or even demonstrations in the street, some of the participants will be exclusively described as being *des intellectuels*. Surely, in the U.S. or the U.K., no one would dare call himself an intellectual: he would have to be further described as a writer or professor or whatever. If you look the word up in a French dictionary, it will say that an *intellectuel* is someone whose life is devoted to *les activités de l'esprit*, i.e., someone who spends his time thinking. There is a well-known story about a famous French thinker, whose name escapes me, who had the word *intellectuel* printed as his job description on his passport and no one found this in the least odd. Why not give it a go when you next apply for one?

SERVICE NATIONAL: National Service no longer exists in France, but it is interesting to know the history of the term and, when I first came here, it was very much a topic of discussion among friends and relatives of my age. As no one was particularly keen to spend a year pretending to be a soldier and putting off the day when they could start earning some money, the main words I heard were those that related to the means for getting out of doing it. One of the words people wanted to hear was *réformé*, which meant that you were excused from your service because you were considered unsuitable in some way: flat feet, asthma, or whatever. Better still was *exempté*, which simply meant that you were excused from National Service on personal grounds but without specifying any shortcomings, whether physical or psychological. This was the ideal escape because there was no adverse judgment of any kind nor stain on your character. The one to avoid was, seemingly, P4, the lowest psychological evaluation, which meant that you were let off because you were frankly too bonkers to be allowed to go. Nevertheless, many young people went to great lengths to pretend that they were potty—favorites included standing on their head for hours or pretending they couldn't actually speak—so that they would be let off as P4. Unfortunately, they forgot that the evaluation would follow them for the rest of their careers. If you couldn't get out of *Service National*, the word most used during the year's service was *la quille*, which meant the end of your year when you were finally set free.

Entertainment and Sport

In this section, we will discover a selection of words relating to various spectator activities as they are enjoyed and practiced in France.

Not only will we find out why going to see pantomimes with French people is a risky business, what a typical French dog is called, and why you should beware if a Frenchman wants to interest you in his chocolate bar, we will see how best to encourage a French sports team and what to do if they win.

Films *and* Cinemas

ATMOSPHÈRE . . . : There are certain film quotes, or fractions of quotes, that you seem to hear remarkably frequently in France. Where I first worked, whenever anyone
used the word *atmosphère*—which means, unsurprisingly,
roughly what it means in English—one or other of my
colleagues would mutter in a fake, shrill Parisian accent,
"Atmosphère, atmosphère . . ." None of my other colleagues
showed any surprise at this nor did anyone think to offer
me any explanation as to why they felt that they had to
do it. After I had heard it several times, I made an effort
to find out what it was all about. It turns out to be part of
a famous quote from a 1938 French film called *Hôtel du
Nord*. This is a place that still exists, standing on the banks
of the Canal St. Martin in Paris. The quote is spoken by
an actress known simply as Arletty. In full it goes, *"Atmosphère, atmosphere! Est-ce que j'ai une gueule d'atmosphère?"*
pronounced in her shrill, authentic Parisian accent. This
translates roughly as, "Atmosphere! Atmosphere! What
do I care about atmosphere?"

BIZARRE: This is the second word that comes from a famous film quote. In the same way that mentioning the word ATMOSPHÈRE prompts people to imitate Arletty saying *"Atmosphère, atmosphère . . . ,"* using the word *bizarre* generally causes someone nearby to say something like *"Bizarre? Vous avez dit bizarre? Comme c'est bizarre."* The line comes from a well-known film called *Drôle de drame* starring Louis Jouvet, who says the line, and Michel Simon. Jouvet actually says to Michel Simon, *"Moi j'ai dit bizarre? Comme c'est bizarre."* You may find that you use the word *bizarre* quite often, so beware! If you get ATMOSPHÈRE and *bizarre* in the same sentence when talking to a group of film buffs, you will never hear the end of it.

MÉDOR: If there is a dog in a classic 1950s British film, there is a fair chance that it will be called Rover. Similarly, in British children's programs that involve farmyard animals, the horse will probably be named Dobbin—and this despite the fact that no living horse is called that, nor probably ever has been—while the cow will be Buttercup. Should there be a cat in a story, it may well be called Tiddles or Whiskers, a hamster, if present, being known as Hammy. The French equivalent of Rover is *Médor*, though I know of no one who has ever met a dog of that name. However, at the time when we drove a Rover car, we though it hilarious to refer to it as "Médor." Extensive research has revealed that a French horse in an old film might well be called Pom Pom, though people seem much more certain that the cow would be called Marguérite. Tiddles, the cat that features in an English film, would probably be known as Minou in the French version. Sadly, there seems to be less affection for hamsters in France because there is apparently no common name for them.

OUVREUSE: You would think that going to the cinema in France would be essentially the same as doing so in your own country. Unfortunately, things are rarely as simple as they seem. The first time I set foot in a French cinema—a particularly flashy one on the Champs Élysées—we were shown to our seats by an *ouvreuse* or "usherette." She had taken the tickets from us at the door and then handed them back by our seats, leaving her hand outstretched. While I was still wondering what the girl was up to, my wife produced a coin of some sort and gave it to her. She accepted it with minimum gratitude and left us. Thus, I discovered that you are expected to tip a cinema usherette. Tipping in cinemas is now limited to extremely fashionable cinemas, but you will definitely be expected to tip in most theaters when seeing a play and even in sports stadiums. A good way of passing the time, while you are waiting for the show to begin, is to watch the patrons as they arrive and see if you can guess by the girl's reaction how much or how little she has been tipped. You will also be able to get a rough idea of how much she earns in an hour and thus understand why jobs as *ouvreuses* in fashionable theaters are much in demand.

Other *Forms* of Entertainment

PANTOMIME: This is a term that exists in French but only to describe a show based on mime. The idea of pantomimes as they exist in the U.K. is quite simply unheard of in France. This came to light when we went with some French friends to a traditional English pantomime in Paris. As we sat waiting for the play to begin, we carefully went through the helpful program notes with our friends Christophe and Hélène to explain the sort of things that you are expected to shout out and at which moments. We made it clear that the choice is limited to comments such as "He's behind you" and "Oh, no he isn't," each of which should only be used at specific moments. They almost, almost grasped it. At a key moment in the play, the wicked Vizir was about to have Aladdin executed and people in the audience, visibly moved, were calling out things like "No! No!" It was at this point that Christophe decided to take his first steps in audience participation, choosing the quietest of moments to call out the immortal words, "Mind ze dog!" The result was astonishing: the actors stopped dead. Silence and confusion reigned both on stage and in the audience, for there was no dog anywhere to be seen. Christophe, oblivious to all this, beamed proudly, the play resumed, and Aladdin, you will be relieved to hear, did not get executed.

TÉLÉVISION : I include this word, not because I believe that you don't know what it means, but rather as a pretext for saying publicly how absolutely appalling French television really is. Indeed, I don't really know which is harder: explaining to French people how awful their television programs are, or persuading British and American people that they should be far more grateful to those concerned for providing the best channels in the world. But back to the essential point: French TV (with the possible exception of the ARTE culture channel) is rubbish. I could give you reasons and examples to support my point of view, but it wouldn't change how bad it really is. So I won't bother. It is not worth it.

Sporting *Matters*

Les bleus: Whatever the sport, be it football, rugby, or basketball, the French national team always wears blue shirts. They are thus, unimaginatively, known as "Les Bleus." Supporters, *L'Équipe* newspaper, and even news bulletins always refer to the performance of *Les Bleus* when reporting on a match. The name features strongly in the all purpose cheer *"Allez les bleus!"* a cry which is particularly useful in that it works for whatever sport you are watching. You can either shout it out on its own when the occasion requires it or, at moments of extreme emotion, you can transform it into a simple and rather repetitive song that goes:

Allez les bleus!
Allez les bleus!
Allez!
Allez les bleus!
Allez les bleus!
Allez!

It looks complicated, but it's quite easy to pick up. It is also streets ahead of the dreadful English football chant that goes "En-ger-land; En-ger-land!"

Colleagues leaving work on the evening of an important match will stick their heads round friends' doors and say, *"Allez les bleus pour ce soir!"* and expect some kind of enthusiastic and confirmatory response.

CHANTS DES SUPPORTEURS: In France true football (soccer) supporters are not much different from their British counterparts when it comes to their conduct while the match is going on: they chant. More particularly, they chant some fairly unflattering things. For example, when a goalkeeper is getting ready to take a goal kick, there is a collective cry of *"Oh! Hisse . . ."* as he takes his run up, followed by a long, drawn out cry of *"Enculés!"* as the ball flies down the field. *"Enculés"*—typing this is a new experience—is extremely rude and means something like "you buggers" and is directed at the opposing fans. When the home team is winning, or has won, the fans taunt the losing fans by singing, *"Et, ils sont où, et ils sont où, et ils sont où les—?"*— Where have they gone?—where the name of the opposing team is put in at the end. Also, when things are going well for one team, their supporters will be on their feet cheering. At this point they chant *"Qui n'est pas debout n'est pas—"*—whoever isn't standing up doesn't support whichever team we are talking about. Lyon supporters have a variant of this idea. Not only do they stand up, they bounce up and down chanting, *"Qui ne saute pas n'est pas Lyonnais"*—whoever isn't bouncing isn't a Lyon supporter. Of course, the poor referee can occasionally get some special attention, especially when he makes controversial decisions. Those unhappy with his efforts shout, *"Aux* CHIOTTES *l'arbitre!"*—stick the ref in the toilet!

CHEVAL: The correct term for "to ride a horse" is *monter à cheval*. There are, however, people who say *faire du cheval*. It is probably not a good idea to lend your horse to that sort of person.

COCORICO: French roosters do not say "Cock-a-doodle-doo" in the manner of their British cousins; they say, *"Cocorico."* More interestingly, French people use *cocorico*, or possibly *coquerico*, as a victory cry. This may well be because the cockerel is the symbol of French sporting teams—this is shown by enthusiastic fans releasing live roosters onto the pitch at major sporting events. Thus, when announcing a victory, a person or a newspaper headline will start with the word *cocorico* before going on to specify what the victory was. *"Cocorico! On a gagné une médaille d'or!"* You can even use the word *cocorico* as a synonym for victory, for example describing an uninspiring victory as *un petit cocorico*.

CYCLISTES: This is not so much a word as a concept that you have to learn early on, especially if you plan on driving anywhere in France on a Sunday morning: cyclists in France are firmly convinced that roads exist for their sole benefit, to the exclusion of all other road users. This conviction is particularly strong on Sunday mornings. Not only do French cyclists resolutely cycle two or three abreast so that they can chat to each other, thus forcing any following car to drive at twenty-five kilometers per hour, but also, and more disturbingly, they believe that their ownership of the road is dependent on their wearing extremely brightly colored and, quite honestly, far from flattering, lycra suits. Pick a bit of road near any sort of greenery on a Sunday morning and you will be amazed by the number of brightly dressed cyclists that you spot. If you can't see any, you will probably hear some because they like to shout to each other, especially when they are out very early in the morning. I have a theory that says that, when I am out cycling in jeans and a T-shirt, the likelihood that another cyclist will greet me, or acknowledge me in any way, is inversely proportional to the brightness of his lycra and the sophistication of his wraparound sunglasses.

FANFARE: If you are going to go to a six-nations rugby match at the Stade de France, try and catch the RER with the brass band in it. If you can't find the car with the brass band, try to get the one with the rooster. The emblem of the French team is a rooster—*le coq*—and one or two fanatical supporters like to travel to the stadium with a live cock which they let loose on the pitch at the start of the game. The poor thing then spends most of the match wandering aimlessly about, dodging balls and charging players, until, apparently, it is recaptured and taken home to recover. It is not clear whether the rooster accompanies the supporters to the bar after the match—see TROISIÈME MI-TEMPS. Finding the car with the rooster is admittedly not easy, unless you are traveling at daybreak. What is far simpler is finding the one with the brass band in it. Each crowd of supporters tends to include at least two *fanfares*—a group of brass-instrument-wielding fans who sit together in the stadium and urge on their team with bursts of strident, cheery music. Like everyone else (including the rooster) they have to get to the stadium by public transport. If you are lucky, you will find yourself in the same train, or better still, in the same coach as a *fanfare* who use the trip out to the stadium as a warm-up period. Even a small brass band can really make its presence felt in a confined carriage, especially when they, and accompanying fans, start bouncing up and down with the beat.

NOUS: Convincing proof, should such really be needed, that the French are more chauvinist than the British is provided by the fact that, whereas the British commentator of a televised sporting event always refers to the home team as "they" or "the British," the French TV commentator says *nous*, or "us."

SPORTS: The only common name of a sport that seems to be exactly the same in French and English is rugby. However, as the word is generally only used by players or commentators who typically come from the far southwest corner of France, it is usually pronounced something like "Rrru-uby." While football is strictly known as *football* in French, hardly anyone, of course, says it. The game is known simply as *le foot*, the game itself being *un match de foot*. Basketball and handball (a game that is widely popular in France but little known elsewhere) have identical proper names in French but again are generally known as *basket* and *hand* so that people go and see *un match de basket* and not *un match de basketball*. The ball itself is not *un football* but *un ballon de foot*. Volleyball, another game that is very popular in France , is known as *le volley*, the ball itself being *un ballon de volley*. Cricket is strictly *le cricket* in French but the only people who pronounce the word are in fact mixing it up with croquet and so don't count. This is perhaps a good moment to give you some excellent advice: never, ever, even think about attempting to explain the rules of cricket to a French person.

TABLETTE DE CHOCOLAT: A splendid example of the different ways we and the French view things! The English (and some Americans, too) are very keen on drinking beer while the French are very keen on sweet things. Thus, while a finely muscled male stomach reminds us of a six-pack of beer, in France it is known as *une tablette de chocolat* or bar of chocolate. Interestingly, overconsumption of either beer or chocolate will make obtaining the stomach in question almost impossible.

TIERCÉ: You have to learn a whole load of horse race–related terms just to be able to sit through the news on France Info, for the evening news bulletins often mention the day's *tiercé* result. Whereas in England you tend to back a single horse to win or place, and refer to it by name, in France, you back horses by referring to their number on the race card, and you also tend to bet in groups. A *tiercé* is a bet on the first three horses in a given race. You thus study the race card, make your choice, and predict first, second, and third by their number. After the race, the announcer will read out the results, saying, *"Les resultats du tiercé à Saint Cloud: le quinze, le sept, et le onze,"* and that's it. No names of the horses at all, and you only win your bet if you have got the three correct numbers in order. If you have the correct numbers in the wrong order, you win less. There are also special races which require predicting the first four or even five horses. These are called *quarté* and *quinté*. Incidentally, most of these races, known as "harness racing" in the U.S., are not run at a gallop on the flat or over jumps, but at a trot pulling a lightweight cart called *un sulky*. If you want to bet on a *tiercé*, you can do it in a special bar for horserace fanatics called a PMU (Pari Mutuel Urbain) though such bars are generally smokier and dirtier than ordinary bars.

TROISIÈME MI-TEMPS : It only takes one expression to show that French rugby supporters are made of different stuff than soccer fans. *Le troisième mi-temps*—the third half-time—refers to the time spent in the pub just after the match has ended. What is important about this is that supporters from both teams get together and enjoy a beer or six without anybody thinking even remotely of beating each other up. This is particularly visible after a six-nations rugby match where the bars near the Stade de France fill up with supporters of both nationalities whose only common language is beer and who, because of this, get along famously. I have often witnessed lone fans ordering rounds of beers in a bar after a good rugby game, sure in the knowledge that like-minded strangers of other nationalities would shortly appear and share them.

VÉLO: Another disappointment: at school I remember learning that the French word for a bicycle was *une bicyclette*. I needn't really have bothered: no one seems to use the word *bicyclette* at all. The two-wheeled device, beloved of lycra-clad Sunday morning sportsmen, is known as *un vélo*. This is an abbreviation of the old word *vélocipède*. A racing bike is *un vélo de course* and a mountain bike is *un VTT*, which stands for *un vélo tous terrains*. This is perhaps a good moment to point out that loads of English books about France and the French will have you believe that a common French term for a bicycle is *la petite reine*, or the little queen. This may have been the case fifty years ago, but it certainly isn't now. Not only have I never heard the expression used by anybody, but a brief survey showed that several French people I asked didn't even know what the term meant.

Les virages: In football stadiums, notably at the Parc des Princes where the Paris Saint Germain team plays, the really ardent supporters congregate in the corners of the stadium. These are where the stadium bends and so, logically, these areas are known as *les virages*—the bends. Depending on who you are, and how fervently you support your team, not to mention how much you fancy a good punch-up after the match, you will either actively seek out, or take great care to avoid, *les virages*.

$\mathcal{P}$APERWORK

If there is one thing that should make you think twice about coming to live in France, it is the paperwork. For there really is an awful lot of paperwork to be dealt with when you live here. If you are unconvinced on this point, you merely have to check the handy guides to all the various cartes *and* permis *that are sold in newsstands and book shops. Of course, if you just come on holiday, you won't need to apply for a resident's permit or an identity card. Furthermore, you will most likely never have a stressful encounter with a French civil servant at his unhelpful best. And what a loss that is!*

This chapter covers French weddings, which may come in handy if you ever find yourself invited to one. Having read it, you will be encouraged to discover that you already have all the French vocabulary you need to get married here yourself, should you wish to. You will also come to understand why the French don't share the British tradition of sending a slice of wedding cake by post.

The section ends with tips on how to sell a car and the real reason why you should give blood in France.

Documents

CARTE D'IDENTITÉ: In France, everyone has to have, and carry, some form of identification. This identification is not necessarily a passport. All French people, whether they travel abroad or not, have to have an identity card or *carte d'identité*. Not long ago, as well as including the holder's personal details such as his date and place of birth as well as a photo, the identity card even included the holder's index fingerprint, something that I found absolutely astonishing when I spotted it on my wife's card all those years ago. Now identity cards are modern, plastic-covered cards that are supposed to be tamper-proof. In the U.K. where you don't necessarily have any official form of identity document, check cards were devised as proof that the person signing the check was indeed who he claimed to be. The person receiving the check just has to compare the signatures on the back of the card and on the check to be sure that all is well. In France, when you pay by check, you invariably hear the cashier ask for *une pièce d'identité, s'il vous plaît*—asking to see some kind of formal identity. This identity can be your identity card, your passport, or your driver's license, or, for very large sums, all three. The cashier then copies down the reference number of the chosen document on the back of the check.

CARTE DE SÉJOUR: At the time of writing this, even if you are a citizen of one of the states of the European Union, you must have a *carte de séjour* or resident's permit for an extended stay in France. In order to get one, you must have been in a job for at least three months as three months' pay slips are required to show regular employment. Once you have these, you also need your passport, some photos, and a phone or electricity bill as a *justification de domicile* to show where you live. You take all these to your local *sous-préfecture* (regional town hall) where you will spend the morning waiting in line and filling in forms. If any of your photocopied documents is not considered up to snuff, you will be sent away to get another one. This means waiting in line all over again another day. Once the form filling has been completed correctly, you will have to wait several weeks for a *convocation*, which is a summons to return to the *sous-préfecture* to do some more waiting and finally be given your *carte de séjour*. This is a plastic card that lists all your personal details and includes the unflattering photo that you provided and which now looks even worse than before. Many years ago, my first *carte de séjour* had the words *"Police de Paris"* conspicuously printed across the top. I used to take great delight in brandishing it in response to a request for some proof of identity, trying to imitate the way policemen on TV flash their identity cards at suspects. It hardly ever impressed anybody.

FONCTIONNAIRE : French civil servants, or government employees in general are known as *fonctionnaires*. They enjoy
a peaceful life, but if threatened in the slightest by proposed
government legislation, they will go on strike, or *faire la
grève* with impunity. True civil servants are referred to as
ronds de cuir, which is a reference to the round leather cush-
ion found on old-fashioned office chairs. As a foreigner,
you are most likely to encounter *fonctionnaires* when you
want to get a CARTE DE SÉJOUR. When you first set out to get
one, I recommend that you adopt the strategy devised by
my wife for getting on the good side of a *fonctionnaire* from
the moment of your first encounter. This consists in saying,
right at the beginning, in as sincere voice as possible, *"Mon
dieu! Vous avez enormément de travail!"*—goodness, you are
extremely busy—whether they actually appear to be doing
anything or not. It works wonders! The collective term for
a plurality of French *fonctionnaires* is *l'administration*. This
all-purpose term covers the civil service and bureaucracy
in general and is generally only heard when someone is
complaining about something.

IMPOSSIBLE: There is an expression that is used to show how
resolute and wonderful the French typically believe themselves to be: it is *"impossible n'est pas français!"*—impossible
isn't the French way. Whenever a person is faced with a
tricky problem and someone suggests that it is impossible,
whoever it is may well use the expression to show that there
is no way in which he is going to give up and be beaten.
However, it seems that only French people are allowed to

use it of themselves; I discovered this when faced with a recalcitrant civil servant—see FONCTIONNAIRE—who was telling me that giving me a resident's permit on the strength of the papers that I had prepared was *"impossible."* Thinking that the expression would provide a splendid and unarguable answer to the woman's objection, I said, *"Mais, je croyais qu'impossible n'était pas français"*—But I thought that impossible wasn't the French way. Instead of being stunned by my logic and erudition and saying that I was absolutely right and that there was no need to fill in any more forms whatsoever, the woman turned red in the face and shouted *"Vous vous foutez de moi?!"*—Are you making a fool of me?—and looked as if she would throw my file on the floor. Apologizing and getting her to calm down and reconsider my file took absolutely ages.

LIEU DE NAISSANCE: There is one main difference that is easy to spot between the numerous French forms that you have to fill in and typical English ones. And it has nothing at all to do with language. For the most part, any French formal document that you are required to complete—and heaven knows, there are a lot of them—will ask you to include in the list of your personal details, not only your date of birth but also your place of birth. Typically, the form calls for *date et lieu de naissance* as soon as it has made clear who is being talked about. In France, your birth certificate, passport, identity card, driver's license and LIVRET DE FAMILLE (see Weddings) all specify your date and your place of birth. Applying for a bank account, joining the local library, signing on at a new school, applying for university, buying a house, and a whole load of other things all require you to tell someone where you were born. As they are going to mention it so often, it is advisable, if you can possibly manage it, to make sure your children are born somewhere nice, preferably somewhere chic and expensive. This will improve their success at practically anything in later life. We managed this brilliantly for our son, who was born in Neuilly—one of the smartest of Parisian suburbs—but did less well for our daughter, who was born in the eighteenth arrondissement of Paris despite the fact that we were living in the more up-market seventeenth at the time.

NOM DE FAMILLE: There seems to be disagreement in France as to which comes first—your first name or your surname. On the ever-present forms that you keep filling in in France, a lot of them specify *"Nom, prénom,"* requiring you to fill in your *Nom de famille* or surname first and your first name second. We could dispute the logic of this, but as it is their country and their forms, we won't, for the moment. At least when it occurs on a form, you can see which name is which, assuming the person has filled in the form correctly. What causes problems is when certain people introduce themselves. For there are a considerable number of people in France who have been brought up to give their surname first, and the first name second when introducing themselves. Thus they say something like, *"Bonjour. Dupont, Jacques."* This is peculiar, perhaps, but not too tricky, because Dupont is a readily recognized surname and Jacques is easy to spot as a first name. What is difficult is being introduced to someone who has a surname that sounds like a first name. There are loads of people with surnames like Michel, Martin, and George that sound like they should be first names. If someone shakes your hand and says, *"Bonjour. Martin, Michel,"* you have no idea whether you are facing M. Martin or M. Michel. Worse, if you make an assumption based on your way of doing things, you may be with someone who assumes the opposite. I had a boss who believed in the surname first technique, while I, resolutely, come from the surname second school. When we were introduced to "Georges, Martin," I spent the meeting thinking I was with M. Georges, but saying nothing, while my boss kept calling him Monsieur Martin. In fact he really was M. Georges!

Weddings

Oui: I include this, not because it has some peculiar or exotic meaning other than the one that you learned at school, but rather because it is the only word that you have to be able to pronounce in order to get married in France. Of course, this only applies if you have a civil wedding at *la mairie*. A church wedding requires considerably more effort on the part of the bride and bridegroom. In a French civil marriage service everything hinges on this single word spoken by the bride and groom. Each party just has to say *oui*, preferably at the right moment, in reply to a long and convoluted question which is asked by *Monsieur le Maire*, and the deed is done. In my case, while I wasn't going to have much to say, I nevertheless wanted my *oui* to be as perfect as possible. So, in the evening of the day before our wedding, I was to be found, or rather, I was thankfully not found, in a distant corner of my future parents-in-law's huge garden saying *oui* out loud in a variety of tones until I hit upon one which sounded assured, positive yet friendly. I'm pleased to say that people commented on it in favorable terms after our wedding.

LIVRET DE FAMILLE: Marriage certificates as such don't exist in France. Proof that you are really married is provided by your *livret de famille*. This is a plastic-covered beige booklet, about the size of a big passport, which is issued by the *mairie* in the locality where you got married. After six pages of detailed notes on how to cope with the formalities relating to the various births and deaths that await you down the road of life, you come to the interesting bit which is the *Extrait de l'Acte de Mariage*. On the left-hand page are given the details of the *epoux*, or bridegroom—his date of birth, place of birth, and the names of his parents. Similar details of the *epouse*, or bride, are given on the opposite page. The date of the marriage is given, though it is generally partially obscured by a large and impressive stamp showing the name of the *mairie* where the wedding took place as well as by the *maire*'s unnecessarily flamboyant signature. At the bottom of the page are shown details of the *contrat de mariage*, or prenuptial agreement, which the bride and groom may have chosen to enter into. This decides how your goods are to be divided up in the event of the death of one of the spouses or of a divorce. Whenever you buy property you will be asked for details of your *contrat de mariage*. If, like us, you decided not to have a prenuptial agreement at all when you got married, you will have to reply to such questions by saying that you are ruled by the regulations known as *La communauté réduite aux acquêts* which I believe means a fair fifty-fifty share out. The remaining pages of the *livret de famille* are for details of the date and place of birth of your children. There is room for up to eight offspring should you be energetic enough as to require it.

PIÈCE MONTÉE: One of the major differences between French and British weddings lies in the wedding cake. You can explain to your future family-in-law—should you be lucky enough to marry a French person—that what you really want is a substantial fruit cake covered in white icing and preferably forming an assembly of three similar cakes of decreasing sizes, until you are blue in the face. You won't get one. What you will get is an extraordinary structure called *une pièce montée*. This is a generally conical shape about eighty centimeters high which is made up of loads of little choux pastry balls filled with vanilla cream and stuck together with sugared icing. It is generally topped off by charming little figures of a bride and bridegroom. When it comes time to eat it, rather than ceremoniously cutting the cake, the bride and groom break chunks off the cake with their fingers and serve it out. Everybody gets about three pastry balls each. It is actually quite good and considerably lighter on the stomach than the British equivalent, especially if you don't try to eat the little figures on the top. The fact that this sort of cake isn't cut into neat parts and has to be eaten on the day of the wedding due to the cream content explains why friends and family in England who couldn't come to our wedding were disappointed that we didn't send them a slice of cake by post as we would by British tradition.

Formalities *and* Institutions

L'ARGUS: The minute people start to talk about buying or selling a car in France you can be sure that *l'Argus* will be mentioned at some point. When I first heard friends or colleagues talking about selling a car and saying, *"Je l'ai vendue à l'Argus"* I wondered who it was or, alternatively, where such a place might be. It turns out that *l'Argus* is neither a fanatical collector of secondhand cars, nor a salesroom. It is a secondhand car magazine, analogous to the *Blue Book* in the U.S., that mainly comprises lists of models of cars, set out by their year of manufacture, and showing their value for a variety of conditions. *Vendre à l'Argus* thus means that you sold your car at the price specified for it in the magazine. Garages that are prepared to purchase your old car when you buy a new one will offer to buy it at *à l'Argus*. Depending on how keen they are to sell you the new one, they will sometimes go as far as offering *Prix Argus plus dix pourcent*, or less, if cars are selling well. The magazine comes out every Thursday.

À jeun: I encountered this when I had to give blood for the first time in France. *"Soyez à jeun,"* it said on the friendly notice in the office calling for volunteers. *Jeun* comes from *jeuner* which means "to fast." *À jeun* therefore means "in a state of fasting" or simply that you shouldn't have eaten any breakfast before you go to give blood. However, there are differing views about what strictly constitutes being *à jeun*. Those who tend to respect rules to the letter take it to mean that you shouldn't eat or drink anything what- soever before doing whatever it is. French people, on the other hand, interpret the term more liberally and assume that, while they shouldn't eat a hearty breakfast, they can surely be allowed a cup of coffee or two to help them cope with the rigors of giving blood, or even just giving a blood sample. Certain medicines specify on the packet that they should be taken *à jeun*. This is generally construed to mean that you swallow them with your first sip of coffee in the morning.

Donner du sang: The large room in the converted to- bacco factory where I used to give blood in Bristol used to be filled on donation day with a number of rickety camp beds. After you had finished giving blood you were led to one of the camp beds and made to lie down. A charming nurse would then bring you a reviving cup of tea and a couple of custard cream biscuits. The plain surroundings and the simple tea seemed to increase the feeling of virtue that you got from doing your social duty. Once you had finished your tea you went placidly back to work. Giving blood *à la française* is not a matter of virtue; it is a gastronomic extravaganza. The blood removal procedure is itself similar to that used in England. The difference lies in what they give you afterward. When you have finished, there is no question of being led to a camp bed. Even less is there talk of cups of tea. The nurse leads you to a table that is groaning under the weight of croissants, BAGUETTES, ham, saucisson, pickles, and tomatoes and, most surprising of all, carafes of red wine. As I generally give blood in the early morning, I don't get much work done before midafternoon.

LETTRE RECOMMANDÉE: It is time for a wild generalization: the French are completely obsessed with sending "certified" letters. The full term for such things is *une lettre recommandée avec accusé de réception* or "a certified letter with acknowledgment of delivery," and they are rarely used for good news. For sending or receiving a *lettre recommandée* is usually the sign that a conflict is looming or that you are in some sort of trouble. Even though a certified letter is considered proof that a letter has been delivered, there are always shady people, or *petits malins*—cunning little guys—who push things to the limit. True *petits malins* have been known to acknowledge receipt of a certified envelope but to maintain that the envelope didn't actually contain a letter at all. Faced with this sort of behavior, someone devised a special certified envelope for hardened *petits malins* where the envelope is made of a sheet of card folded in two. You write the text of your letter on one side of the card, then fold it and glue it closed. The whole thing is then stamped, addressed, and registered. As the envelope *is* the letter, it is impossible for even the most duplicitous addressee to deny that he has received the contents. The sight of a *lettre recommandée* can cause fear and trembling, even in those who have nerves of steel. The bell rang one Saturday morning and I opened the front door to see our postman, Marcel, at the front gate brandishing a large brown envelope. *"C'est une letter recommandée,"* he called cheerily. Before I could answer, or start walking toward him, Marcel continued in a calming, reassuring tone, *"Mais, c'est vos chequiers. Ce n'est pas le Fisc"*—"It's your checkbooks; it's not the tax people." Having a clear conscience, it hadn't occurred to me that it might be the *fisc* and I was surprised that he felt the need to mention them. So I asked whether people generally assumed that registered letters came from the tax people. Marcel animatedly explained that if he didn't tell people who the registered letter was from, they invariably panicked, assumed it was from the income tax people, and ran off to hide in their houses. He also said that if people were out when he called, he would leave a card saying that a certified letter was waiting to be picked up at the post office, but that he always wrote on the card who the letter was from; otherwise people wouldn't come and collect it. According to Marcel, this sort of thing happens a lot in our village because of the number of rich people who live there.

LIVRET A: A staple of French life. Almost everyone has one. *Un Livret A* is the basic sort of French savings account. You can open one either at the equivalent of the post office savings bank—known simply as La Poste—or at the national savings bank which is called *La Caisse d'Épargne*. Intended principally for small savers—the maximum you can save is 15,300 euros—a *Livret A* won't make you rich as the interest rate is currently just two percent. It is, thankfully, tax free. This is not the case with other savings accounts. The main advantage of *Livrets A* is that people feel safe with them, mainly because their parents probably had one. Also, they are really easy to open and often come with a cash card for easy withdrawals.

MARIANNE: If you go into the *mairie* of any French town or village, you will spot a bust of an attractive woman in a prominent position on a plaque or on the wall above the *maire*'s desk. This is Marianne—symbol not so much of France but of the French Republic. She first started to appear in *mairies* on the centenary of the French Revolution in 1889 when she was created by a sculptor called Injalbert. Marianne is invariably represented wearing the woolen cap that was worn by women during the revolution and which is known as a *bonnet Phrygien*. Before the introduction of the euro, you saw Marianne far more often: she was depicted on the back of the one franc and five franc coins as well as on all the old PIÈCES JAUNES. You now only generally see her as a stylized image on French postage stamps. In order to keep her as contemporary as possible, and to maintain public enthusiasm, new busts are regularly produced based on whichever beautiful French woman is currently in the public eye. Recent Mariannes have been modeled on Brigitte Bardot, Catherine Deneuve, and Laetitia Casta. The more recent the bust, the bustier it seems to be!

SDF: This stands for *sans domicile fixe*—with no fixed abode—and is the generally used term for a homeless person. People refer to *un SDF* and can be heard observing, for example, that *"il y avait un SDF dans le train ce matin."* Using the full name, rather than the letters, can lead to misunderstandings. One winter four of these unfortunates froze to death in the streets in Paris. The news bulletin referred to the death of *"quatre sans domicile fixe"* which several people, including me, misheard as "quatre cents . . ." assuming that four hundred people had died! If he should take to begging, a homeless person transforms from an SDF into *un mendiant*.

THE CALENDAR YEAR

Travelers in France don't limit themselves to the summer holidays anymore: visitors now seem to take weekend breaks all the year-round. With this in mind, I have set out words that relate to things that happen on various days of the week, as well as throughout the year. The Christmas and New Year period in particular has events and traditions that have no equivalent in other countries. And did you know that in France there are several days in addition to your birthday and Christmas when you receive presents from your family and friends? This may be one good reason to pick up and move to France.

We will also see why you shouldn't worry if the air raid sirens suddenly go off (assuming you are on holiday on a Wednesday) and which day you should try to be in France if you want to increase your chances of being kissed on the cheeks.

Times *of* Day

LE MIDI: This is a commonly used term for a time of day that, according to certain people, does not actually exist. In French, a normal day can be broken down into *le matin* or *la matinée* in the morning; *l'après-midi* in the afternoon; rounding off with *la soirée* in the evening. By extension of this practice, many people use the term *le midi* for "lunchtime." Purists however, will have none of this and maintain that there is no such expression as *"le" midi*, believing that anything that happens around midday happens *"à" midi*. Thus, one group will fix an appointment, planning to do something *le midi* while the others will meet up *à midi*. The people who say *le midi* are also the sort of people who say *manger* and will therefore issue invitations for lunch by saying, *"Si on mangeait ensemble ce midi."* Those who eschew *le midi* also will have nothing to do with *manger* and have to be more clear, and more long-winded, about their invitation. They thus say something like, *"Si nous déjeunions ensemble aujourd'hui."* The *le midi* camp has a disctinct advantage in that their term covers any time from around twelve to just after two. If whatever it is doesn't happen at precisely midday, the *à midi* lot have to use another expression such as *l'heure du déjeuner,* which can be inconvenient. The principal disadvantage of *le midi* is that it leads to constructions such as *un midi* or "one lunchtime." Unfortunately, this can be misheard as *à midi*, which can lead to disappointment when vague invitations to have lunch one day—*"si tu venais manger un midi"*—are misheard as the more definite *"si tu venais manger à midi."* Incidentally, the term *le Midi* is also a perfectly correct way of referring to the south of France, people going to spend their summer holidays *dans le Midi.*

The *Days* of the Week

BONNE FÊTE: This was a term that I discovered on November fourth in the first year I lived in France. Arriving at work, I met my secretary in the corridor who, instead of giving me her usual firm handshake and brief *"Bonjour Charles. Ça va?"* cried cheerfully, *"Ah! C'est votre fête aujourd'hui!"* She then kissed me soundly on both cheeks, exclaiming, *"Bonne fête!"* The fourth of November turns out to be the feast of St. Charles. In France, almost every day of the year is associated with a given saint in the Roman Catholic church. The names of the saints correspond to the most frequently used French first names. For example, September tenth is the feast day of Ste. Inès. Most diaries and desk calendars show the name of the saint whose feast day or *fête* is celebrated on each day of the year. It used to be that when choosing first names for children born in France, you were only allowed to choose from the list of names that appeared on the calendar. This limited the number of first names one was likely to encounter, but at least it avoided children the embarrassment of being subjected to outrageous invented names or being given the names of all the players on a winning football team. However, not all days of the year have an associated first name. Some public holidays shown in the calendar are just called by their title such as *Fête du Travail* for the May Day holiday. There are tales of children of immigrants whose parents understood the principal of picking names from the calendar, but unfortunately picked July fourteenth as their inspiration, their poor children being forced to grow up being called *"Fête Nat"* or "national holiday." A final, important point is that, if you are French, not only are you wished *"bonne fête"* on your feast day by members of your family, and kissed on the cheeks by all and sundry, they also tend to give you a present. It is worth moving your family to France just for that.

JOUR FÉRIÉ: There are far more public holidays—*jours feriés*—in France than in other nations. It is a simple matter to check that list which they print in diaries showing the dates of the various public holidays in countries around the world. According to my diary, whereas in the U.K. the number of public holidays is nine, France enjoys fourteen. Only Switzerland, with eighteen, has more. All these

French public holidays fall on their particular calendar date and not always on a Monday as public holidays do in the U.K. and the U.S. Thus, a given public holiday will fall on a different day each year, and the movement of public holidays leads to the creation of long weekends—see PONT. The French have historical *jours fériés* on November eleventh and May eighth, to commemorate the end of the First and the Second World Wars, respectively. The rest of the holidays are French Catholic religious feast days, which are not celebrated in the U.K. or U.S. Ascension and Assumption celebrate the ascension to heaven respectively of Jesus and Mary. *Pentecôte* is the day of Pentecost, when the Holy Spirit came to the Apostles, and *La* TOUSSAINT is All Saints' Day.

MERCREDI: *Mercredi*, which, as I am sure you know, means Wednesday, is interesting in that it is the day of the week when new films are released at the cinema. As the new films come out that day, Wednesday is also the day that magazines such as *Pariscope* are published. *Pariscope* is the most popular of the various magazines that give the details of cinema programs in the Paris area, as well as information on theaters and museums. A great Parisian tradition consists of buying *Pariscope* each week, studying it, marking the various films, exhibitions, and plays that you plan to see that week, and then not actually going to see them. This is great fun, and particularly good value as *Pariscope* only costs forty centimes. *Mercredi* is also the most popular day of the week with young French schoolchildren because it is traditionally the day of the week when there is no school. Children have Wednesday off, but make up for it by having school on Saturday morning. Finally, the first Wednesday of every month is special in France because at twelve noon on the dot all the air raid sirens are tested. For a whole minute (which is a really long time when you are subjected to a World War II air raid siren just outside your window, as I am) the sirens wail their warning. Then, once you have got your concentration back, ten minutes later they sound the all clear for another thirty seconds.

The *Year*

CARTES DE VOEUX: These are greeting cards, more specifically the sort that you send to friends around the Christmas period. In the U.K. it is traditional to make every effort to send your cards—which we tend to call "Christmas cards"—early enough to be sure that they are received before Christmas day. Indeed, people in the U.K. are often quite irritated by cards that arrive after Christmas, as they tend to assume that they have either been forgotten by the sender or that the sender only sent the card in reply to the one received. In France, you don't have to rush to send your cards because they are not thought of as Christmas cards at all. They are rather seen as New Year's greetings cards and, as you are wishing people a Happy New Year, there is no point sending your card before the end of December. Most

French people believe that *cartes de voeux* can be sent at any time up to the end of January. Unfortunately, in French offices, they tend to apply this principal to greetings cards sent to U.K. associates. I have tried several times to instill a sense of urgency into the sending of cards to the U.K. by my colleagues, but with no real success.

ÉTRENNES: Some people have all the luck. In certain, essentially Catholic, French families, you not only get a present on your birthday, at Christmas, and on the day of your *fête*—*see* BONNE FÊTE—you also get a present for your *étrennes*. This is a small New Year's present that is typically only given by immediate family to their children or grandchildren. Nevertheless, when I first met someone around New Year who was brandishing the present that he had received for his *étrennes,* I confess that I felt a bit jealous. This guy got presents on twice as many occasions a year as me! However, the more common meaning of *étrennes* is "Christmas box." In the weeks before Christmas a seemingly endless procession of people will ring your doorbell and expect to be given a small financial gift to mark the festive period. These will include some or more of the following: the postman; the garbage men; the local firemen; the local policemen; and the road menders, known as *les cantonniers*. Some will give you a receipt, supposedly so that you can write off the sum on next year's taxes. Others will give you a Christmas card with a festive message and a calendar. The more generous will give you a proper calendar, generally bearing a large and brightly colored photo of a festive kitten. Experience shows that in late November it is a good idea to prepare an envelope near the front door with appropriate sums of cash ready, as well as a pen to note who has been tipped that year. Secondary visits, whether intentional or not, are not uncommon and should be rebuffed with a firm *"Mais, vous êtes déjà venus."* Certain miserly householders are rumored to try this on the first visit!

NOËL: When, in my twenty-second year, I set out to spend my first ever Christmas in France, I was prepared for loads of things to be completely different. I had, however, somehow assumed that Christmas would at least be celebrated on the same date as in England. This assumption proved to be misguided as the Christmas meal—see RÉVEILLON— turned out to be planned for the evening of December twenty-fourth. Cautious inquiries about exchanging presents lead to more surprises. This was to take place at the very end of the meal, around midnight. Further questions about possible substantial lunches on the twenty-fifth were met with incomprehension. Nothing was planned for the twenty-fifth at all! I have since discovered that there are numerous French families who give their presents on Christmas morning, the twenty-fifth, but that such families still have their Christmas meal on the previous evening. Nevertheless, my first December twenty-fifth was spent with neither a huge meal, nor any presents, and not even a James Bond film on the TV, and it was a sorry affair indeed.

PAQUET CADEAU: This term, which literally means "present package," is French for "gift wrap." It is a splendid aspect of French culture and is something that I never imagined existed until the day I first went to buy some perfume for my wife. Once I had ordered what I wanted, the sales clerk inquired, *"C'est pour offrir?"* wanting to know if the perfume was intended as a gift for someone. Wondering what business it really was of hers, I just mumbled something indistinct, whereupon she set about wrapping the perfume with expensive paper, lengths of ribbon, and gold sticky labels. The resulting package was a masterpiece. And there was no extra charge. Gift wrap is all part of the service. In the pre-Christmas run-up, most French shops do gift-wrap more or less automatically. There are often special counters just after the cash registers where there are girls who do nothing but gift-wrap. It is traditional to tip such girls, provided that they make a good job of it. If the shops are too big, or too busy, they generally provide lengths of branded wrapping paper, or colorful envelopes, for customers to take away with their purchases so that they can wrap them at home. The only problem with this kind of paper is that the person receiving the present will spot straight away where you have bought it, and thus start to try to guess what it might be.

RÉVEILLON: A key word to learn if you are going to be in France over Christmas and the New Year. The French most often celebrate Noël on the evening of December twenty-fourth. The occasion around the huge Christmas meal is known as *le réveillon*. People leave the office early on the afternoon of the twenty-fourth, saying things like, *"On va féter le réveillon chez mes parents,"* and head off to the station. There is also a verb *réveillonner,* which quite logically means "having a huge meal on December twenty-fourth." However, things being never simple, the word *réveillon* is disconcertingly ambiguous. As well as referring to the huge meal that is eaten on December twenty-fourth, the term also applies to the huge meal that is eaten on New Year's Eve. For no family New Year's Eve celebration would be complete or even possible without at least a four-course meal including some or all of the following: oysters, foie gras, smoked salmon, a roast of some sort, a selection of cheese, a chocolatey dessert, and loads of wine. Champagne, of course, is served at the stroke of midnight. The generic expression for Christmas and New Year's Eve together is *les fêtes*. People agree to meet up, for example in January, *après les fêtes*.

TOUSSAINT: This is the day of the year that falls on November first, when everybody remembers the dead. When you visit a cemetery in England on any given day, you are likely to see one or two graves with recent flowers, several graves with faded or fading flowers, and the majority with no flowers at all. This sporadic presence of flowers around a cemetery is explained by the fact that, while many people visit family graves regularly, most people tend to lay flowers on their relatives' graves only on the anniversary of their deaths or on some other anniversary such as a birthday. Thus, I suppose, only one grave in every 365 receives fresh flowers on any given day. In France, while people may visit their relatives' graves in the course of the year, they will, almost without exception, also visit the graves on La Toussaint. Thus, November first is a day noted for the amount of traffic on the roads, and, sadly, the number of road accidents, as people return to their childhood homes to lay flowers on family graves. Not only does practically everybody choose that single day of the year as the day on which they have to visit a cemetery and lay flowers, but also tradition has it that only certain varieties of flowers are suitable for such use. You can basically choose between carnations and chrysanthemums. Flower shops all over France stock up on these flowers in the last days of October each year so as to be ready for the rush. Of course, despite the fact that November first is a public holiday, most flower shops will be open, at least in the morning. The graveyard, which slopes up the hill behind our local church, is quite crowded from mid-morning onward on November first. There are a few people who come alone but the majority comes in family groups to place new flowers and generally tidy the graves.

Annual *Events*

PIÈCES JAUNES: Before the arrival of the euro, French franc coins included the five, two, one franc, and fifty centime coins, all of which were shiny silver colored. The remaining coins, those of lesser value, the twenty, ten, and five centimes, were made of golden colored alloy and were known as *les pièces jaunes*. Desperate beggars would encourage you to give them any amount, however small, with the words, *"J'accepte même les pièces jaunes."* There is a traditional annual operation to raise money for children's hospitals which involves leaving decorated cardboard charity boxes in public buildings, post offices, and schools into which people are encouraged to put their spare change. This event is known as *Opération Pièces Jaunes*. It was started in 1989 and is presided over by Bernadette Chirac, wife of the former president. It is a very popular event during which much-publicized trains travel the length and breadth of France collecting literally tons of coins. The operation is mainly directed at children. Euro coins also include *pièces jaunes*, but their value is considerably higher than their franc counterparts.

LES SIGNES DU ZODIAQUE: The signs of the zodiac are another source of confusion when you start learning French. I had assumed that, as all the names of the signs appear to be classical in origin, they would all be roughly similar in French. Only one, Cancer, is exactly the same in both languages. Some of them are almost the same, such as Saggitaire, Taureau, and Scorpion. But poor Libra, Pisces, Capricorn, and Aquarius are unrecognizable, becoming respectively Balance (because of the scales), Poissons, Belier, and Verseau. Luckily, horoscope pages of French newspapers include the dates to which the signs apply so that you can quickly track down the right one. Virgo gets a special mention because in French it is *Vierge,* which means "virgin." Asking Virgo people what sign they are is particularly entertaining because they have to answer, *"Je suis Vierge"*—I am a virgin—and may even blush.

How to Sound French

I have to admit that the title of this section is, perhaps, a little optimistic. For a start, I know all of these words and no one has ever suggested that I sound French. What is more, I have no real reason for assuming that you actually want to sound French. Nevertheless, I have always believed it is better to aim higher rather than lower. So, even if you don't end up actually being taken for a French person, this selection of words should at least help you to stand out from the run-of-the-mill crowd of tourists. And that is probably achievement enough for many of us.

But back to the words. They cover such a broad range of subjects that they haven't been grouped together but are simply set out in alphabetical order. You will find words that don't mean quite what they seem, words that cause problems even for French people, and a couple of English first names that might be misconstrued in France.

BRAVE: There are two French adjectives—the other is GENTIL—that at first sight seem to mean something kind and friendly, but which in fact can have the opposite meaning. At school you learn that the French word *brave* means "courageous," "gallant," or just plain "brave." However, you can hear people who are clearly neither brave nor gallant nor even less courageous being described as *il est brave* or *c'est un brave homme* by people who are obviously not trying to be flattering. The clue is in the tone of voice. This usually tends to sound insulting or at best patronizing. *Il est brave* means roughly that he is a nice enough fellow who is basically harmless, but that you shouldn't expect too much from him. I had a colleague who could best be described as wishy-washy, of whom all that my other colleagues could say was that *"il est brave"* in a sneery sort of voice while shaking their heads sadly. This term seems to be most often applied to men.

CERTAIN: An odd word in that its meaning changes according to whether you stick it before or after a noun.

If you put the adjective before the noun, it adds a notion of vagueness to whatever it is; if you put it after the noun, things become much more definite. For example, an elderly person could be described as being of *un certain age,* which means he is quite old but could still be expected to get full value from a new magazine subscription, while saying that they are of *un age certain* means that they are really old and decrepit. This effect leads to people echoing a phrase that someone has said including the word *certain* but reversing the position of the word to add emphasis. For example, when something has been causing you problems you might say, *"J'ai connu une certaine dificulté,"* whereupon the person you are talking to responds, *"Ou une difficulté certaine,"* and smiles knowingly to show that the difficulty that you were faced with was tougher than you are letting on.

CHEZ: You would not believe the problems that can be caused by this simple, short word. There is no literal translation for *chez*, but it roughly means "at the place or home of." You probably know that "our house" is *chez nous.* Similarly, people who are going home say, *"Je vais rentrer chez moi,"* and there is nothing wrong with that. Problems arise, not when people say *chez* but when another word is used instead. Going to the dentist, the doctor, or the hairdresser should be described by using the word *chez* as in *"Je vais chez le medecin"* or *"Je suis allé chez le coiffeur."* Unfortunately, some people use *au* instead of *chez* and say, though it causes me real pain to write this, *"Je suis allé au* *coiffeur"* or *"Je vais au dentiste."* Hearing this dreadful mistake hurts more than having your teeth drilled.

CONDAMNÉ: This word means "sentenced" or "condemned." However, confusingly, you often see signs on doors which read *"Porte condamnée."* When I saw one of these for the first time I wondered what the poor door had done to be punished like that. In fact *condamnée* in this context means "blocked off" or "sealed off" and the sign is simply there to stop you wasting your time shaking the door handle and vainly trying to open it. The door hasn't actually been punished at all!

COUVENT/COUVENT: These two words, which appear to be identical, are included as examples of the duplicity of French pronunciation. In all fairness, the majority of French words are pronounced as you would expect. *Couvent* is a nice example of a word that, according to its meaning, can be pronounced quite differently. When it is a verb—the third person plural of the present tense of *couver*, which is the act of sitting on its eggs by a hen—it is pronounced "coove." *Couvent*, however, can also be a noun meaning "nunnery" or "convent." In this case it is pronounced "coove-en." Thus, laying hens in a convent would be described as *les poules couvent dans le couvent*, with the identical words being pronounced quite differently. This is about as hard as pronunciation gets in French, but, it must be admitted, is kids' stuff compared to "Slough, cough, bough, chough, through, and though" which together can make foreign students give up and leave English-speaking countries forever.

CUCUL: If, when faced with this word for the first time, you happen to know that the word *cul* is particularly rude and means "arse" or "ass," you may fear the worst when someone is described as being *cucul*. In fact, it is a fairly innocent slang word that means "wishy-washy." An uninteresting, rather prim and fussy girl, the sort of girl that you definitely wouldn't go and flirt with at a party, will thus be described as being *cucul* or, inexplicably, as *cucul la praline*, where *praline* normally means a crunchy, sugared almond sweet. As with many of the adjectives described here, *cucul* is not one that you want to hear used in relation to one of your friends or family.

D'ACCORD: An omnipresent word. Indeed, most French people would be incapable of having any sort of discussion without it. The expression *être d'accord* means "to agree." Of course, people don't say, *"Je suis d'accord"* any more than English speakers say, "I agree with you." They just say *"D'accord"* in the way we say "okay." When you hear someone on the phone setting up an appointment, you will hear the words *d'accord* spoken increasingly often as the two people reach agreement on what they are going to do and the conversation draws to its end. This end is generally marked by a decisive *"Ça marche!"* which means something like, "That's fine." Of course, using the final *"Ça marche!"* does not preclude using *d'accord* a couple more times afterward, just to tidy things up. There are those who think that *d'accord* itself is too long and shorten it further to *d'acc*. The opposite of *je suis d'accord* is *je ne suis pas d'accord*. This is rarely shortened to *pas d'accord* except when presenting a debate, summing up the opposing positions as *d'accord* and *pas d'accord*. If you get fed up with saying *d'accord* more than twenty times in a long conversation, you can always vary things a bit by using *entendu*—"understood"—a few times.

DE: When you want to make clear that something belongs to someone, this is the word used to indicate possession in French. The famous first phrase that you were supposed to learn at school was *la plume de ma tante*. In general terms, therefore, the thing belonging to someone is *le truc de quelqu'un*. Unfortunately, not everyone says *de*; a fair number of people say *à*, saying *la voiture à Paul* rather than *la voiture de Paul*. This is a heinous error and should be avoided at all costs because you really don't want to sound like the sort of person who makes this kind of mistake. The only time you are allowed to say *à* instead of *de* is when you are blaming someone. In *Les Misérables* by Victor Hugo, Gavroche says: *"C'est la faute à Rousseau . . . c'est la faute à Voltaire."* Victor Hugo, of course, knew it was a mistake. French people imitate Gavroche and say something like *"Ce n'était pas moi: c'est la faute à Pierre."* This is okay because it is clear that you are making a famous literary reference. Some people say *à* instead of *de* for all sorts of things and when you remonstrate with them, will try and justify themselves by referring to Gavroche. Do not be fooled: they really are making a mistake.

DONT/QUE: Take heart! You are not alone. French people make mistakes too when speaking or writing French. One of the most common is putting *que* where they should put *dont*. As a general rule, *dont* takes the place of *de quoi* and is used with verbs that are followed by *de* such as *se souvenir de* for "remember." There are several common expressions which require the use of *dont*, for example, when being scared of something. This is *avoir peur de quelque chose*. But when you turn it around to say "What I'm scared of is . . ." it should become *"Ce dont j'ai peur . . ."* Unfortunately, certain people (and it is always the same sort of people as in other examples elsewhere in this book) say, *"Ce que j'ai peur . . ."* This is quite simply appalling. If you should hear someone say this, or *"ce que je me souviens"* instead of *"ce dont je me souviens,"* feel free to berate them most forcefully. The fact that it comes from a foreigner might just make them change their wicked ways.

EN REVANCHE: I include this not because it is particularly interesting but because it was one of my first boss's pet obsessions. There are two ways of saying "on the other hand" in French. One is the more commonly used *par contre*; the other is *en revanche*. Purists heap scorn on *par contre*'s head, accusing it of being semantically incorrect and common. Others believe that there are certain, clearly defined contexts where you should use one or the other of the two expressions. Unfortunately, when questioned, such people can never explain what these circumstances actually are. Nevertheless, after working in an environment where *par contre* was more or less forbidden on pain of receiving an irritating reprimand, I have forever forsaken it and now only ever say *en revanche*. Feel free to use whichever one you choose, but you can't go wrong if you always say *en revanche*.

ESPACE: *Espace* just means "space" or "room" but, over the past decade, it has come to be used to try to make practically anything sound smarter and more trendy. If in doubt, stick the word *espace* at the beginning of whatever it is you are about to use. It is the word that is really *à la mode*, or fashionable. The meeting room at work has been refurbished and is no longer known as *la salle de reunion*; it has a bright new label on the door that reads *"Espace Reunion."* Similarly, what used to be a *zone fumeurs* or smoking section, is now an *espace fumeurs*. The word *espace* seems to be chosen to make whatever place is concerned seem modern and cool and up to date. This doesn't always work, for example, when the grubby corridor with the coffee machine at work was relabeled *"Espace Café."* The word also crops up outside the office. The village meeting hall in the town where we live is now, apparently, referred to as *l'espace culturel* or "culture space." It still feels just like a village hall, though.

FOIE/FOI/FOIS/FOIX: Four words that sound exactly the same. One means "liver," one means "faith," the third is "time," and the last is the name of a town in France. When you hear someone exclaim *"ma foi,"* you can deduce that he is talking about his faith and not his liver because *foi* is feminine while *foie* is masculine. Not to mention the fact that exclaiming about one's liver would be odd, even for a French person.

I learned a poem at school which is intended to help remember which is which. It goes:

> *Il était une fois*
> *Un homme de foi*
> *Qui mangeait du foie*
> *Dans la ville de Foix.*

> *Il se dit "Ma foi!*
> *C'est la première fois*
> *Et la dernière fois*
> *Que je mange du foie*
> *Dans la ville de Foix."*

GARE!: *Gare* with an exclamation mark after it has nothing to do with *gare* without an exclamation mark. You probably know that *une gare* is a railway station—in my first French textbook, people spent an inordinate amount of time asking the way to the nearest one. Knowing this, I was perplexed to read a newspaper headline which proclaimed, *"Gare aux explosions!"* because it seemed to have nothing to do with stations. *"Gare!"* means "watch out" and comes from a verb *se garer* which generally means "to park your car" but in this context means to watch out for, or to avoid something. A painter would urge you to mind the wet paint by saying, *"Gare à la peinture!"* while an irritable parent would tell a young child to do something and back it up with a threat to *"Gare à toi"* or worse, *"Gare à tes fesses,"* warning them to watch out for a smack. You might think that you should say *garez!* to someone you say *vous* to, but *gare!* is an interjection, and not an imperative, so you don't. If you do something spontaneously, or without warning, you do it *sans crier gare!*

GENTIL: This is the other of the two French adjectives that, while it can be applied in a friendly, flattering way, can also be applied to mean something less complimentary. In its polite sense, it means "kind" or "nice." You can thank someone by saying, *"Merci. Vous êtes très gentil"* or observe some act of kindness with the words *"c'est gentil"* and no one will take offense. You can even compliment someone on their charming home by describing it as *"C'est gentil chez vous,"* but I wouldn't necessarily want anyone to say that about our house. Where things start to go downhill is when you are describing someone—of course you never say it to their face—and say something like, *"Il est très gentil, mais . . ."* or simply *"Il est gentil . . ."* in a sardonic, whiny tone, while adopting some kind of sneery expression. Said like that, *gentil* is used to convey the fact that he is a nice enough person, I suppose, but that is really all that can be said about him. Not bad for a short, simple word.

GLACE SANS TAIN: The main reason I'm including this is because I find the French term and the corresponding English one equally annoying since neither describes what the thing in question really is. The English term is a "two-way mirror" but that is exactly what it isn't. You can only see through it from one side; from the other side, you can't see through at all because it is shiny. If you could see through it both ways, there wouldn't be much point in having it and it would be called a window. The French term is equally annoying because it literally means "mirror without silvering" but the mirror *does* have silvering, or rather does have the modern equivalent thereof. If it didn't, it wouldn't look like a mirror from the side where you can't see through it. I feel much better for sharing this with you! Thank you.

H: The letter *h* is a tricky one in French, especially when it comes at the beginning of a word. For once a word starts with an *h*, the problem of elision starts to raise its ugly head. Elision, the carrying over of the sound from the end of one word into the start of the next word, is a perennial French problem. If you are faced with the words *les haricots* you have to decide whether you should say something like "lay aricots" or whether you can be sloppy and get away with "lez-aricots" with the *s* of *les* sliding into the beginning of *haricots*. In this example, you quite definitely have to make the effort to go for the "lay aricots" version. This is specified clearly in all the books and backed up by l'Académie Française and you don't want to get on their bad side. In the better dictionaries, the phonetic spelling of the word has a little apostrophe before it to show that you have to say "lay" and not "lez" beforehand. Other words such as *hôtel* are the opposite. Saying "lay hotels" sounds silly. You are thus free, indeed are encouraged, to say "lez-hôtels." The question of elision before an *h* is an important one. Occasionally, French people stop in mid sentence and inquire, *"Est-ce que l'on dit 'lez-hirondelles' ou 'lay hirondelles'?"* which generally leads to collective disagreement and the person forgetting what he was originally talking about. For some words it becomes very tricky indeed. These are the words where elision used to not be allowed but for which, inexplicably, l'Académie Française has had a change of heart and said that you now can. There are even words for which l'Académie can't make up its mind and just suggests that elision might be allowable but is really frowned upon in the best circles. An example of this is the word *handicappés*.

HARO: I include this word because I once sparked off a fairly acrimonious dispute between two complete strangers sitting either side of me on a plane simply by asking what on earth it meant. It was in a headline on the front page of a paper which read simply, *"Haro sur le gaspillage."* The *gaspillage* bit was okay. I knew that it meant "wastage." The *haro* part caused more problems. One neighbor claimed that it was a cry for help in time of robbery, where any person hearing it became entitled to arrest the perpetrator. This turns out to be true, but it wasn't the sense in which it was used in the article. The other claimed that crying *haro* was a sign of reproach or condemnation of the thing in question. This seemed to fit the headline better. Inexplicably, both of them kept saying, *"haro sur le baudet"*—a *baudet* being a sort of donkey. To my frustration though, neither of them could explain what the expression meant nor, more interestingly, why they both knew it.

INVARIABLE: Just when you start to get the hang of French, you come across the notion of *les mots invariables*. Practically every French word gets an *s* on the end in the plural—apart from the ones that get an *x* like *chou* or *cadeau*. There are exceptions to most rules and the exceptions in this case are *les mots invariables*. These are words whose singular and plural forms are the same. It must be said that there aren't many of them, and what's more, they are not things that you talk about all that often. For example, there is the word for "lampshade," *abat-jour*. If you have one it is *un abat-jour* and if you are lucky enough to have three, it is *trois abat-jour*. Similarly, one windscreen is *un pare-brise* while two cars between them have *deux pare-brise*. The only good thing about all this is that if you say the words, rather than write them, no one will know whether you are aware that you are dealing with such complex vocabulary. Unfortunately, now that you do know them, no one is going to know either.

-MARIE: Very few English men are called Mary. Similarly, Marie is principally a girl's name in France, whether alone or in compound names like Marie-Claire or Marie-Béatrice. But, strange as it may seem, it can also appear in male compound names. You have only to think of M. Le Pen. His first name is Jean-Marie. If anyone thinks ill of him, it probably isn't only because of his name. You can also encounter people called Pierre-Marie or Paul-Marie. Such names are usually a sign that the person comes from a particularly devout Catholic family. When I first encountered a Jean-Marie, I thought it was hilarious that the poor bloke was called Mary. Unfortunately, no one else seemed to think it was odd at all, so I laughed alone. While it is fairly common for men to have compound names ending with Marie, no male has a name beginning with it: this is reserved for women. On the other hand, men do suffer the indignity of having compound names that begin with Ange, or Angel. I recently met an Ange-Dominique and was much amused by the name. Again, I laughed alone, because it is apparently a typical Corsican name, and you really don't want to upset a Corsican. Finally, you can combine Marie and Ange to get the woman's name Marie-Ange. Perhaps this is indicative of coming from a devout Corsican Catholic family?

ON: You could probably write a whole book just about this single, short word. Its uses are numerous and its strength can be surprising. At its simplest level *on* means "one" or "someone." An unknown person punching you in the street would be described as *on m'a frappé*. More commonly *on* means "us" in that it takes the place of the word *nous* in all sorts of sentences, such as *on est allé au restaurant*. If this statement is given in answer to a question to a couple along the lines of "What did you do this weekend?" it is clear that the *on* refers to the two members of the couple. However, *on* can be used to preserve secrets or to avoid divulging information. The same question, "What did you do this weekend?" addressed to someone who doesn't speak about their personal relationships will lead to exactly the same answer—*"On est allé au restaurant"*—but this time, the *on* can mean absolutely anything from "the entire French Olympic weightlifting team and I" to "my secret lover and I" to the more mundane "my parents took me out to lunch but I don't want to admit to it." The word *on* can be used to give instructions to someone while making it clear that it doesn't much matter who does it, the only important point is that it won't be the person giving the instructions who actually does anything. Discussing the need to write a letter, my current boss will say in his particular fashion, *"Il faut qu'on écrive une lettre."* This means that someone has to do it, but it clearly won't be him. If there are two or more people involved, no one will know who should be preparing the letter, even though everyone will know who won't be doing it. You can also use *on* to claim undeserved credit for something done by others. By saying, *"On a obtenu un contrat très important,"* you can try to imply that you were involved in the negotiation of the contract, even though you were on holiday at the time. Fortunately, this tactic doesn't always work.

PAF, PAN, PLOUF: Learning a foreign language is a long and exhausting business. Not only do you have a huge number of words to master, you also have to learn the various onomatopoeic sounds for everyday events. By this, I means words like "splash," "bang," "crunch" that are used to show what kind of sound occurred. You only have to look at an Asterix cartoon book to see that all the sound words are different in French. Someone falling into water goes "splash." In France, they will get just as wet, but will go *"plouf."* Being hit in the face with a large fish goes *"paf"* in French where it would go "smash" in English; slamming into something goes *"vlan"* instead of "slam" while a short sharp hitting sound is *"poc."* A quick look at any episode of Tintin shows that French guns don't go "bang" but rather pathetically just go *"pan."* There is also a wonderful word for falling over and hurting yourself, which is *"badaboum!"* Small children describe their falling over by saying, *"J'ai fait badaboum!"* while parents, observing their offspring smacking into the tarmac will say helpfully, *"Oh! Badaboum!"* as though the child might not have been aware that he had just fallen over. Finally, it is as well to know that when you have been struck by something that goes *"paf,"* you should cry out, *"Aie!"* rather than "Ouch!" or no one will come and comfort you.

PAS ÉVIDENT: In French *évident* means "obvious" or "clear." The word, however, seems to be used more often in a negative sense in the form *pas evident*. While this literally means "not obvious," the term implies that whatever task we are talking about is particularly tricky and should be expected to cause some difficulty when it comes to dealing with it. Asking a plumber whether he can fix something will lead to much sucking of breath and a discouraging *"C'est pas evident."* This, of course, doesn't mean that he won't be able to fix it. Rather, it is intended to make you understand how grateful you will be expected to be once he has fixed it. It is not only the person faced with the task who is allowed to say, *"C'est pas evident."* Any bystander or spectator of a slightly pessimistic nature will invariably lower your enthusiasm for the job at hand by a shake of the head accompanied by a despondent *"C'est pas evident."* Such people are usually somewhat disappointed when you actually accomplish the task.

PAVILLON: One of the first French words anyone ever learns is that for a house, which is *une maison*. It turns out that there are far fewer *maisons* in France than might be supposed. What there are lots of are *pavillons*. Though this word looks like it might mean "pavilion" and imply something rather grand, it is in fact just the common word for a small, modern house set in a bit of garden and sitting between two identical other houses. A series of *pavillons* all together is *une zone pavillonnaire*. Somehow, therefore, the word *pavillon* is less flattering than *maison*. I always refer to the family home as *notre maison* and try never to use the word *pavillon* at all. When you have something delivered, the man in the shop always asks, *"Vous êtes en appartement ou en pavillon?"* in order to have some idea of how many steps and other obstacles may be encountered. I tend to resolutely reply, *"En maison."* Young married couples in France dream of moving into a brand new *pavillon* that they have just had built, more or less to order. During the period when the *pavillon* is being built, they will proudly boast to all and sundry that *"on est en train de faire construire."* The fact that the product being built is a *pavillon* is so obvious that the word doesn't even need to be mentioned.

PÉTER: It is not necessarily a good idea to go and live in France if your first name happens to be Peter. For *péter*, albeit with an accent on the *e*, means "to fart." A fart is *un pet*, a word that I once managed to confuse with *une pie*—a magpie—and produce a shocked, collective silence at a christening party, for Monet did not paint any pictures of farts.

The verb *péter* is quite handy and can be used for a broader range of things than just passing wind. The explosion of bombs and other noisy devices is described as *péter* as are the bursting of zippers and the splitting of seams. Busting pretty much anything, from a vase to your nose, can also be defined by use of this practical word: *"Je l'ai pété."* But its scope is broader still. If you drink too much, you can be described as being *pété* somewhat in the way that an English person would use the word "pissed." You can, if you like, draw parallels between this expression and the British expression "pissed as a fart." Finally, you can even make up compound words like *pète-sec* which, rather than relating to farts, defines someone who is bossy and sharp tongued.

Incidentally, there are girls' names, too, that may cause misunderstandings in France, notably Penny. Penny sounds uncomfortably similar to the French word *pénis* which means exactly what it looks as though it means.

PETIT: You could probably write a thesis on the way the word *petit* is used. In its basic sense it just means "little" as opposed to "big." But what is much more interesting is the way that it is used to encourage someone to accept something. To understand what I mean, you just have to go to any restaurant in France. Whenever the waiter suggests that you might like to have anything over and above the basic minimum, he will define whatever it is as being *petit*. At the beginning of the meal, before you have ordered, he will ask if you want a drink. But he won't say, *"Voulez-vous un apéritif?"* he will say *"Voulez-vous un petit apéritif?"* By doing so, he will suggest that it is not unreasonable, nor in any way extravagant, to order one, and that no one will think any the worse of you if you do. There will then be silence on the *petit* front until the end of the main course whereupon the waiter will inquire, *"Un petit dessert?"* Of course you will have a *petit dessert*—being *petit,* it can't be too fattening or too expensive, and the kind waiter is merely doing you a favor by reminding you of this. After you have finished your dessert, the friendly waiter will use the word one last time by suggesting *un petit café.* I have never, ever been offered just *"Un café?"* in a restaurant, but when I have asked waiters why they use the word *petit* like this, none of them admits to doing it consciously. You can also use the word *petit* at home to modestly announce the wine that you are going to serve to your guests at a meal. By calling it *un petit vin* you make it clear that it is not a hugely expensive, famous-name affair, but rather a modest but good quality wine that you have selected for their especial consumption.

PHOTOGRAPHE: This is one of the dirtier tricks that the French language comes up with to upset foreigners. If you were faced with the term *un photographe* what would you think that it meant? I would imagine that, like I did, you would assume that it was the French for a photo. But no! It is French for a photographer. If you say, as I once did, *"Il y a beaucoup de photographes dans mon album,"* people will be most surprised and wonder how on earth you manage to carry it around. The correct word for a photo is *une photographie*. This is generally shortened to *une photo*. Another common word for photo that also causes confusion among foreigners is *un cliché*. If someone offers to show you their *clichés*, I don't know what you might imagine but it probably wouldn't be holiday snaps.

QU'À CELA NE TIENNE: I include this for the simple reason that when I heard it the first few times, I was convinced that it was a single word. My colleagues used to pronounce it so fast that it was impossible to identify any of its constituent words. For quite some time, I thought that part of it was "Aslan" and that thus they were invoking some fictional deity. In fact, as you can see, it is several words, albeit put together in a way that makes their meaning impossible to guess. I'm still not sure what the expression literally means in French. In English, though, the equivalent seems to be "no problem" or even, in some circumstances, "so be it."

RADIO: Of all the French words that you have to learn, the easiest are those beginning with X—they are the ones which are most likely to be exactly the same in both languages. Take for example *xenon*, *xenophobe*, or *xylophone*. They are all, give or take an accent, the same in both. There are two main exceptions. One is the drink sherry, which is *xeres* in French. The other came to light when I heard someone say that they were off to Paris *pour une radio*. When they later returned empty-handed, I expressed commiseration that their shopping trip had come to nothing. However, my commiseration turned out to have been misplaced because the *radio* in question was not the transistor device which lets you listen to the BBC news. My colleague had in fact gone for an X-ray, in French known as *une radio,* short for *radiographie*. The rays themselves, however, are *rayons X*.

RHUME: *Avoir un rhume* is to have a cold. However, French people, or possibly just Parisians, rarely seem to use the word, apparently believing that it doesn't sound serious enough. They tend to go to their doctor and return proudly announcing that of course it wasn't a cold but that they are suffering from *une rhinite, une trachéite,* or, better still, something with a long and impressive-sounding name like *un rhinopharangite.* The longer the name given to the complaint, the longer the illness seems to last and the longer and louder the victim complains about it. Being sublimely indifferent to the fact that, whatever you call it, the illness is of viral origin, and thus completely immune to antibiotics, the sufferers will loudly consume *mes antibiotiques* at mealtimes. Speaking from painful experience, it is not a good idea to try to point out to the sufferer that the antibiotics will in no way act on his viral infection. You run the risk of a sharp reply such as, *"Alors, tu en connais plus que mon médécin?"*—so you think you know more about it than my doctor?

SALON/CHAMBRE: *Une chambre,* as you undoubtedly learned at school, means "a bedroom." However, you quite often hear people saying that they spent the weekend going round the furniture shops to buy *une nouvelle chambre.* Visions arise of them coming home in a big truck with an extra room that they somehow manage to add on to the structure of their house. In fact, *une chambre* in this context means a collection of matching bedroom furniture, typically all bought at once in the same shop. Should it be a set of furniture for a child, when the child grows out of it you can see ads for simply *une chambre d'enfant* in the secondhand column of newspapers. The only detail provided will be the style, typically described as *pin,* or pine, or, my pet hate, *rustique moderne*, a vile term which really means that the furniture is cheap, badly made, and intended to have a vaguely country-antique look about it. The word *salon*, which means "living room," can similarly be applied to a collection of furniture suitable for such a room. Some people try to make their furniture sound even more chic by calling it *un living* instead of *un salon*. Both of these are terms that you should understand if you hear them, but never say.

SCOTCH: Yet another source of confusion: the word "Scotch" used by a French person generally refers not to whisky but to transparent adhesive tape. Such tape is referred to in this way due to the name of its brand, Scotch. I still remember the first time a colleague came into my office declaring, *"Je cherche du Scotch. Est-ce que tu en as?"* and I wondered whether he had taken me for a closet alcoholic. Scotch whisky, by the way, is just known as *du Whisky*.

SI/SI . . . : Two more words that sound the same but have quite different meanings. The simpler one of the two just means "if" and doesn't require any further explanation. The other *si* has no direct equivalent in English. In French there are two degrees of "yes" words—an ordinary one, *oui*, and an emphatic one, *si*. In English, if someone phrases their question in a negative way, for example, "Didn't you enjoy the film?" the person has to make their reply more forceful by saying, "Yes, I did" instead of just "Yes." Alternatively, you accuse someone of not having done something, for example, "You haven't finished your homework," and he or she may reply, "Yes, I have." In French, in reply to a negative question, or an accusation, you reply, *si* rather than just *oui*. Getting it wrong, for example replying to the question, *"Tu n'aimes pas le couscous?"* by a simple *"Oui, oui"* sounds, apparently, particularly odd to French people, who can't understand why the existence of two words for the same thing could cause anyone any problems.

SYSTÈME D.: Another enlightening view of the French character, as seen by the French themselves. As well as being convinced that *"impossible n'est pas français,"* the French are also convinced that one of their essential characteristics is their ability to find ingenious solutions to problems that would confound anyone else, more precisely those unfortunates who are not French. When faced with some problem, people will say that they will have to resort to *système d.* to solve it. But what is this *d?* There is a verb starting with *d* that means "to find a way around problems," which is *se débrouiller* and you may be led to believe that this is the *d* in question. However, this is not the case. The true word is much more vulgar—*se démerder*—which literally means "to get yourself out of the shit." This is why you have to use an initial letter for the verb. Those rare people who actually are good at sorting things out and making a go of it are referred to as *démerde*. You may be recommended to go and ask a particular person for help because *il est très démerde*. Such people are generally quite handy to have around when there is something to be done.

TAPIS: The English word "carpet" can be used quite happily to cover both a wall-to-wall carpet and the sort of free-standing carpet that could also be viewed as a big rug. In French, the word *tapis* that you learn at school as a word for "carpet" in fact only covers the free-standing separate sort of carpet, the kind of thing that North African rug sellers still hawk from door to door. Wall-to-wall carpet has its own name. It is *moquette*. If you tell someone that you have *une nouvelle moquette*, they will immediately assume that it is wall-to-wall. There doesn't seem to be a word for "rug." You have to call it *un petit tapis*. By the way, under the Pont Alexandre III in Paris, there is a sign, now sadly painted over, which used to tell passersby the one thing they were specifically forbidden from doing under the bridge—beat carpets!

TRENTE-TROIS: Ask an English person how old Christ was when he was crucified and they very probably won't know. On the other hand, perhaps because France is a Catholic country, most French people know that he died at the age of thirty-three. This came to light on my thirty-third birthday when practically all my colleagues, on learning my age that day, declared, *"Ah! L'age du Christ."* It is interesting to note that Christ is called *le Christ* in France, which explains why it is *l'age du Christ* and not *l'age de Christ*. *Trente-trois* also crops up in a medical context. When a doctor asks to look at your throat in the U.K., you typically say, "Ahh!" In France, for reasons that have never been satisfactorily explained, it used to be traditional to say, *"Trente-trois!"*

TUTOYER : One of the main differences between French and English, and one that makes life needlessly difficult for a foreigner, is the fact that the French have two common forms for addressing someone as "you." While you can say "thee" and "thou" in English, you generally confine their use to when you are addressing God. For day-to-day use, you just make do with "you." In French you have the choice between *vous* for when you are speaking to someone you don't know very well, or with whom you have a formal relationship (see VOUVOYER), and *tu* for when you speak to friends and family. Talking about whether you say *tu* or *vous* to someone is such a common subject that the French have devised a handy verb *tutoyer*, which simply means "to say *tu* to."

TUYAU: *Un tuyau* is a length of pipe or tubing, the sort of thing that connects your tap to the water main. It is also a useful term to know in the French world of "it's not what you know but who you know," because it means a helpful tip or hint that someone more knowledgeable is prepared to share with you. When reviewing for an exam, a friend may come up and say, with the pride of one who knows something interesting, *"J'ai un tuyau pour l'examen"* before going on to tell you that he knows from some source or other that there is going to be a question about Russian history. In this sense, it is privileged information, something that you shouldn't be expected to have. You can also ask people whether *"vous avez des tuyaux?"* about a confidential subject or about some practical task that requires helpful advice. For *un tuyau* also covers things like do-it-yourself home improvements or cookery. Whatever the subject, you should expect to do better at it if someone gives you *un tuyau*. If the advice turns out to be no good, the information becomes *un tuyau crevé* or "a burst pipe."

VERSION: There are loads of English words that don't have a direct French translation and thus require a description in a dictionary. A simple example is "pith," which, if you look it up in a dictionary, says something like *"la partie blanche de la peau d'une orange."* This sort of word gives you the opportunity to point out, as annoyingly as possible, how much richer is the English language than the French one. However, in the spirit of fair play (for which I am well known) I would like to mention *une version* and *un thème*. While we can only talk about "doing a bit of translation for homework," the French have these two cunning words that tell you whether the work was translated from French or into French. Thus *une version* is a translation exercise from a foreign language into French, while *un thème* is a piece of work going the other way.

VIVEMENT: This sounds as though it ought to mean "lively," which indeed it does. So, when a Truffaut film called *Vivement Dimanche* came out, I assumed it must be about a Sunday when particularly lively things happened.

It was only later when I heard someone say, *"vivement le weekend,"* when clearly looking forward to it, that I began to suspect another meaning. In fact *vivement* can also mean "roll on" or "hurry up." So people are heard in June to say, *"Vivement les vacances,"* or, when they are exhausted at work after a bad day and can't wait for bedtime, *"Vivement ce soir que l'on se couche."*

VOUVOYER: We have seen that there is a handy French verb, TUTOYER, for "saying *tu* to someone." There is an equivalent for the times when you want to make it clear that you say *vous* to a person; this is *vouvoyer*. There is, of course, a word corresponding to *tutoiement* which, you won't be surprised to learn, is *vouvoiement*.

French *Foreign* Words

BILINGUE: I can feel myself getting annoyed already. This word irritates me enormously. *Bilingue* obviously means "bilingual" and should be a word that defines someone who is equally at ease in two languages. If you are not born into a bilingual family, it is going to take a good seven years' hard study to get more or less bilingual, if you are lucky. What I find intensely annoying is the way the word is misused, generally by the parents of French young people who go off and spend a couple of weeks in the U.K. doing a summer job. Once they return, their accursed parents drive everyone to distraction describing their offspring as *bilingue*. How on earth they can believe that two or three weeks working in a pizzeria in Basingstoke is going to make someone bilingual is beyond me. Then there are the parents who say, *"Maintenant, il est bilingue"* and follow this with a self-satisfied, liquid sucking noise where air is drawn in through the teeth. Try as you might, you will never convince such people of their error, even by talking English to the poor offspring and making it clear that they can't understand a word that's being said. When I do this, they usually say that he or she isn't used to my accent. Finally, there are the French people who do a degree in English and think that this makes them internationally renowned linguists. Doing *une licence d'anglais* is generally a soft option at a French university and doesn't require much knowledge of English. When someone says smugly, *"J'ai une licence d'anglais"*—I have a degree in English—I tend to say, "Don't worry, there's no need to apologize." Unfortunately, they tend to look at me as though I am mad.

BYE-BYE: It is surprising how rarely you hear a French person say *au revoir* as our first French classes taught us that they should when saying good-bye. The height of fashion, or of cool, in France seems to be to show off the many foreign words that you know for taking your leave. One of the most common, especially among women, is to say "bye-bye" in a silly French accent. This can even be combined with a French word to give us expressions like *allez, bye-bye* or *Bye-bye, bon weekend*, which is half of one and half of the other. French people with an affinity for things German, or perhaps Alsatian, will say *Tchüss*. If they opt for this, while they don't try to sound a bit British when saying "Bye-bye"—at least I don't believe that they are trying—they will do their best to sound at least a bit German when they say *Tchüss*. Another common practice is to finish off with *ciao*. I have a colleague who gets somewhat carried away and says, *"Ciao, bye-bye,"* when she leaves every evening. There are even those who, inspired by the real Italian farewell *arrivederci*, think it is most amusing to say *"Arrivé d'air chaud."* As this means "hot air inlet," it isn't that amusing at all.

DÉBUT: Can I just ask you, when using this French word in English, saying, for example, "Jack Smith made his début as a singer back in 1981," that you pronounce it "déb*u*" with a short, tight *u*, and not "daybooo" as is so often heard on the BBC? Thank you.

FAKE ENGLISH WORDS: I don't really know what else to call these words. There are quite a few words that are used in French and that seem to be English words, but are in fact slightly odd. The most common of these words is *parking*, which is the French for "parking lot." French people are convinced that it is the proper English word and will happily use it when speaking English, for example when asking of a friendly Londoner, "Can you show me the way to the parking?" There are several fake English words in the field of sports, most notably *un tennis man* for a male tennis player, and *un record man* for a world record holder. People who go running for pleasure refer to this activity as *faire un footing*. However this is quite ambiguous because other people use the same term to mean just going for a brisk walk. Try as you like, you won't convince any French person that any of these are not the proper English words for the things in question. There are also some odd plurals in this category, for example where a plurality of English police officers are referred to as *des policemans*. My favorite one of all was used by my dear sister-in-law, who was considering adopting *un boat people*.

MORCEAU DE SUCRE: As we have seen when dealing with those who claim to be *bilingue*, French people often overestimate their abilities in English. Being only human, I often feel the urge to bring such people down a peg or two. A good way to do this, should you seek to do likewise, is to ask such a person how you say *un morceau de sucre* in English. Ninety-nine times out of a hundred you will be rewarded by a smug smile and the person saying, "a piece of sugar," "sugar" being pronounced with a very long *a*. "*Eh, non!*" you can then say. "*Pas du tout*—it is 'sugar lump,'" before leaning back contentedly and enjoying their confusion.

VO/VF: When a French cinema is showing a foreign film, the program and the sign outside the cinema will specify either VO or VF. These stand for *version originale* and *version française* respectively. *Version originale* means that the film will be shown in its original language with French subtitles, while *version française* means that it will be dubbed into French. Obviously, wherever possible, we go to see films *en VO*. The only problem is that you find yourself spending the whole film reading the subtitles as well to see whether they have translated things properly and thus, occasionally, find that you have got behind with the plot. Seeing the film *en VF* is worse, though, as you find yourself trying to lip read what was actually said. I can generally only do this for the rude words.

Historical Matters and Perfidious Albion

You will be relieved to discover that there is only really one important date that you need to know in all of French history. You will also be treated to a sometimes painful look at how the English are seen by the French. Scottish readers, on the other hand, will have a much easier time of it.

Other topics include an insight into what the French national anthem, "La Marseillaise," is really all about and who became famous just for saying "Non!"

England *and* the English

ANGLAIS: The adjective used to describe any inhabitant of any country of the U.K. French Anglophobes—yes, there really are such people—tend to apply it to any visitor from any English-speaking nation, or, in extreme cases, from any foreign nation at all, except possibly Germany. For example, in a sporting event between England and France, problems can arise when the referee is Irish. Explaining to people that the Irish referee comes from a completely independent country, as different from England as Sweden is from France, falls on deaf ears. Such explanations will not stop virulent allegations of bias based on the fact that the referee is *anglais*, possibly because you can hear him speaking English.

ANGLETERRE: The French seem to have problems when it comes to naming the extensive landmass and its neighboring islands that lie between Calais and Iceland. We know this territory to be called "the United Kingdom of Great Britain and Northern Ireland." The French think it is called *l'Angleterre*. While they know that countries such as

Scotland and Wales exist, indeed they can use these terms quite correctly in the months of January, February, and March when the six-nations rugby championship is going on, they inexplicably tend to refer to these countries at all other times as *l'Angleterre*. Any reasonable list of fruitless things to try to do in France must include trying to explain to a French person the difference between *La Grande Bretagne* and *le Royaume Uni*. This is even harder than explaining the rules of cricket.

L'ENNEMI HÉRÉDITAIRE: The hereditary enemy. This means the English, by the way.

"MESSIEURS LES ANGLAIS, TIREZ LES PREMIERS!": This is one of those quotes about the English that French people know but which is almost unknown in England: my more erudite colleagues say it to me quite often. It seems that at the start of the battle of Fontenoy in 1745, one of the major battles of the War of Austrian Succession, lengthy civilities including much raising of hats were exchanged between the English and French commanders. After finally replacing his hat, the French commander, Charles Hay, the Comte d'Auteroche, is reputed to have cried out this invitation to the English troops to shoot first. The strategic advantage of such an invitation is unclear in that a thousand French troops fell at the first English volley.

PERFIDE ALBION: It came as a considerable shock to discover, in the course of the first months I spent in France, that the country of my birth is not called L'ANGLETERRE as I had for so long assumed. When talking about it, as they very often did, my colleagues referred to it exclusively as *la perfide Albion* or "perfidious Albion." Obviously, they weren't using the term as a simple synonym for L'ANGLETERRE because it implies a fair degree of criticism that really can't be conveyed just by the word ANGLETERRE, however nastily you try to pronounce it. Whenever I tried to argue that the English weren't that perfidious, my colleagues came up with numerous, incontrovertible examples of historical events which clearly showed that we are. The inhabitants of *la Perfide Albion* remain, however, *les anglais* and not, as might be assumed *les perfides Albionnais* or some such.

ROYAUME UNI: Unknown country, occasionally confused with L'ANGLETERRE.

Preferred *Nations*

AULD ALLIANCE: While the English are L'ENNEMI HÉRÉDITAIRE or LA PERFIDE ALBION, the Scots are viewed in a far more favorable light. This is a result of a long-standing friendship between France and Scotland which started in the thirteenth century. Both Scotland and France were having trouble with a belligerent England so it seemed wise that they join forces against a common foe. This was formalized in October 1295 and became known as the *Auld*

Alliance. The effects of this alliance carried on well into the sixteenth century. Nowadays, you only hear it mentioned during the six-nations rugby championship when both countries try their best to beat England. There are times when I take advantage of the fact that my dad was Scottish and, when faced with an unusually Anglophobic French person, claim to be Scottish rather than English. It works a treat!

LES BELGES: Continuing the European theme, *les belges* are the Belgians, a people who enjoy a particular reputation with the French that it would be uncharitable of me to discuss here. The reason I mention things Belgian is that several French icons are in fact Belgian. For a start there is Hergé, the creator of Tintin comics, which are famous in France. He was Belgian and, incidentally, created his *nom de plume* by taking his initials, G. R., and putting them backward to make R. G., which, when pronounced in a French accent, gives Hergé. Not a lot of people know that! Then there is the renowned rock star Johnny Hallyday who not only has Belgian roots, but is, at the time of writing, actively trying to obtain Belgian nationality. Raymond Devos, the great comedian, was born in Belgium as was the singer Jacques Brel. I believe that most French people, if asked, would be convinced that all of these people are truly French.

Historical *Matters*

ANCIEN COMBATANT: While there is no way that I am going to bore you by discussing French success or failure in the various wars over the past thousand or so years, I do think that you should know this term. *Un ancient combatant* is a war veteran or an ex-serviceman. This term seems to crop up more often in France than it does in the U.K., where it mainly gets used on Remembrance Day. For a start, in most forms of public transportation in France there are seats reserved for any ex-servicemen, should there be any traveling. Should someone wish to claim one of these seats, he will have to brandish a card called *une carte de priorité* in order to persuade whoever is sitting there to give it up to him. The few surviving veterans of the Great War are affectionately known as *poilus*—hairy men—because, apparently, of the difficulty they had shaving in the trenches. Those who were wounded in conflict are also entitled to priority seating and, more usefully, parking, but have to show a card or have a sticker on their car that proves them to be GIG, or *grande invalide de guerre*.

JEANNE D'ARC: Six hundred years after her death, she is still the subject of acrimony between the French and the British, or, in my experience, between the French and me. The number of times that colleagues have reproached me with the words "*Vous avez brûlé Jeanne d'Arc*"—the *vous* in question hopefully meaning the English generally and not me personally—is considerable. Trying to explain that it happened in 1431, and thus might no longer be a topical subject for discussion, falls on deaf ears. Similarly, trying to pin the blame for the sorry affair on the Burgundians, and not on the English, won't do you any good either. You really can't forgive things like that. If you are accused of having, in some small way, participated in the burning of poor Joan, the only thing that seems to shut people up is to ask them to remind you when, exactly, it all took place. As they won't know, but won't want to admit it, they will usually change the subject fairly rapidly. In case you are interested, it was May 31, 1431. If you want to know what she looked like, there is a splendid gold statue of our Joan on horseback in Place des Pyramides opposite the Louvre, even though she was burned at the stake in Rouen. She has also, in some way, ended up as being the mascot for the French National Front party, which is possibly less glorious than the statue.

MARIGNAN 1515: The one date that all English people are supposed to remember is that of the Battle of Hastings—1066. Despite the fact that the Norman king William set sail from Dives in Normandy, the French generally have never heard of 1066. The one and only historical date that everyone in France seems to know is the Battle of Marignan, 1515 (pronounced *quinze cent quinze*). What is generally less well known—I have conducted a survey on your behalf—is where Marignan actually is. Lots of people think it is near Marseille because they mix it up with Marignane, which is the Marseille airport. In fact Marignan is just outside Milan in Italy. The battle was fought, and won, by King François I of France, who led his army over the Alps to fight the Swiss who were the allies of Pope Léon X. This was quite a feat because François had only just become king at the tender age of twenty-one. Having beaten the Swiss, François had a chance encounter with Leonardo da Vinci and persuaded him to return with him to France, where Leonardo participated in the design of Château de Chambord which François was having built, and where he lived out his life. This explains why Leonardo died in Amboise and not in his native Italy.

"LA MARSEILLAISE": "God Save the Queen" is Britain's charming and pleasant national anthem which calls on God to take care of the monarch, which, I am sure, He is glad to do. It has served Great Britain well for a considerable period of time. The French national anthem is called "La Marseillaise," and it is a song that was written in 1792 by Claude-Joseph Rouget de Lisle, a Captain of the Engineers in the Rhine Army. At that time, France had just declared war on Austria and Prussia and the army was preparing to go to Paris. The mayor of Strasbourg approached de Lisle about composing a marching tune for this march to Paris; de Lisle apparently composed it that very night. The fact that the song was composed to inspire troops to defeat the enemy comes to light when you translate the words into English. A charming and pleasant anthem it is not. The first verse contains lines like:

"Do you hear in the countryside
The roar of these savage soldiers
They come right into our arms
To slaughter our sons and our wives."

Cheery stuff. But it gets worse when you reach the chorus. This ends with the following:

"March on, March on!
May their impure blood
Water our fields."

Just bear this in mind when you next watch an international sporting event on the television and you see eighty thousand spectators lustily crying for blood.

NAVARRE: This is a name which is only ever mentioned in the expression *de France et de Navarre*. People declare that they have the best job, the finest house, etc., in all of France and Navarre. Most of them have no idea where Navarre is or why it should so generously be included in French territory. Navarre is actually a Spanish province that lies south of the Pyrenees and has the city of Pamplona as its capital. In 1589, Henry III of Navarre became king of France as well as of Navarre and thus became the first of several kings to be known as *roi de France et de Navarre*. Thus, he went from being known as Henri III of Navarre to the better known Henri IV of France. The whole territory was referred to as France and Navarre until the Navarre bit was handed back to the Spanish.

Non!: The most famous French use of the word *non* is in reference to Charles de Gaulle—who is often referred to as *"l'homme qui a dit 'Non!'"* While Charles de Gaulle said *"non"* to a variety of things, his first and most famous *non* was in his speech known as *l'appel du dix-huit juin* in 1940 after the French surrender. He said: *"Mais le dernier mot est-il dit? L'espérance doit-elle disparaître? La défaite est-elle définitive? Non!"* And, in fact, luckily for him, he was right!

$\mathcal{Y}$OUNG PEOPLE (AND THEIR SLANG)

Young people need a section all to themselves. Having learned how to refer to both girls and boys, we will see the sort of slang terms that they use. Of course, many of the words are used by older people as well, even by parents.

You don't necessarily want to say all of these words in public—you have your image to consider, after all. I just want to improve your chances of understanding what the teenagers standing behind you in line for the bus are actually going on about. Unfortunately, they might only be talking about toilets or cigarettes.

For those who have been waiting impatiently, there will at last be a couple of rude words.

Young People

FILLE, MEUF, NANA: The proper word for "a girl" is *une fille*. Several girls together are *les filles*. Young people tend to say *une nana* instead of *une fille*, boys saying things like *"T'as vu la nana là-bas? Elle est chouette!"* or, when announcing a new girlfriend, *"Je viens avec ma nouvelle nana."* The French craze for backslang, known as VERLAN, has produced a new word for "girl." Begin with the word for "woman," which is *une femme* and by applying the "turn it round backward" principal of backslang, *une femme* becomes *une meuf*. You thus hear young people talking about a party where there had been *beaucoup de jolies meufs*.

Dictionaries claim that girls can be referred to as *souris*, or mice, but I have never heard anyone say this.

LES FILLES! LES GARÇONS!: The French seem to have a whole range of ways of greeting several people at once which don't seem to have an equivalent in English. A girl will greet a number of other girls collectively by saying, *"Salut, les filles"* or encourage them to hurry up and leave by yelling, *"Eh! Les filles! On y va?"* whereas in English saying

"Hello, girls" or "Come on, girls" sounds like you are at a ladies' hockey match in Cheltenham. Similarly, a group of boys can be hailed or greeted as *les garçons* or, more probably, *les mecs* by a girl or a boy. You can even greet a group of your friends by saying, "*Salut, les copains*"—imagine walking into a pub and saying, "Hello, friends!"

MEC, GARS, TYPE: We have seen that there are slang words for "girl" in French. By far the most common French word for a "bloke" or "guy" is *un mec*. The late, somewhat lamented comedian called Coluche started most of his jokes with the words "*C'est un mec qui . . .*"

Interestingly, the word *mec* can be used to convey the fact that the man in question is particularly virile and gets respects from his peers simply by referring to the lucky chap as *un vrai mec*. Alternative words for "bloke" are *un gars* and *un type*.

Slang *and* Other Useful Words

À POIL: A handy term with two principal meanings. While *un poil* means "a hair," *à poil* doesn't mean "hairy" as one might assume. It means "stark naked." Thus, you can be caught *à poil* or spend a week in a naturist colony *complètement à poil*. You can also make handy compound expressions such as *se mettre à poil*, which means to get all your clothes off. Apart from the stark naked meaning of the expression, you can also shout it out, for example to your friends, generally when you are outside and in a state of inebriation. Alternatively, you can use the term to great effect by shouting it out in a theater or nightclub where you want to insult the performer and get him off the stage. In either case, *à poil*, when shouted out raucously, means "get off" or "get 'em off," depending on the circumstances involved. It is important not to confuse *à poil* with *au poil*, which means "just right" or "exactly." Even less should you confuse it with *à la poêle*, which sounds very similar but means "pan fried."

BD: Walk round any French bookshop—known as *une librairie* despite the fact that this might make you think of a library—and you will spot a huge range of comic books in quantities far greater than you would ever see in the U.S. or U.K. Comic books are known as *bandes dessinées* but this is almost always shortened to BD. Practically all young people and many adults are addicted to BD. I don't just mean the Asterix series or the Lucky Luke books: there are dozens of titles to choose from. As well as BD for children, there are a whole range for adults, some of which can be surprisingly violent or almost pornographic. Take a trip to la FNAC, a popular store in France, and you will be astonished by the size of the BD section and by the number of people standing around happily reading their way through them. La FNAC occasionally organizes days where the author of a popular BD comes to sign copies of their latest book. On such days, the shop is absolutely packed.

BORDEL: An excellent word with all sorts of handy meanings. In its literal sense, *un bordel* is a brothel and is obviously connected with the word "bordello." However, brothels are clearly considered chaotic by the French, for the word also means a complete mess or a cock-up. When faced with a teenager's disgusting bedroom you could cry, "*Quel bordel!*" or, if you are convinced that some kind of plan is going to go badly wrong, you could predict the disaster with the words, "*Ça va être le bordel!*" Similarly, a long time spent stuck in a horrendous traffic jam could be described as "*C'était vraiment le bordel.*" You can also use the word "*Bordel!*" as a sort of punctuation word to end an exclamation or an order to give it extra weight. Faced with a group of shouting, angry people, you could attempt to calm things down by yelling, "*Aretez de crier, bordel!*" The use of the extra word makes your instruction last longer and so gives it more force. It won't necessarily work any better, though.

CHIOTTES: It is time to descend to things lavatorial. The correct word for a lavatory is *les toilettes*, a word that doesn't seem to have the social stigma of the English word "toilet." The dictionary term is *un lieu d'aisance* but this is never used in real life. As well as these, there are probably as many slang and familiar words for the lavatory in French as there are in English. Perhaps the most common, and certainly my favorite, is *les chiottes*. The equivalent rude term for lavatory in British English is "the bogs," and the French term is amusing because it is the feminine form of *chiot*, which means "puppy." When my parents-in-law bred dogs, there was much hilarity when someone rang up looking for a bitch puppy and inquired, "*Vous avez des chiottes?*" Another word is *les cabinets*, giving the expression *allez aux cabinets*, which is generally most often used by children. All these words, as you will have noticed, are plural. Going well down the social scale, you come to *les waters* a term that clearly comes from WC. The letters WC are also used in France but tend to be pronounced "vay say" and not "double vay say" for reasons that I have never established. If you are trying to be genteel about the thing in question, you can opt for *le petit coin* or "little corner," which is a rare singular term. Finally, many families seem to have their own word for the loo: my first boss went *aux wouah wouah* while others adopt a modified form of the word *cabinets* and go *Aux cabes*. Sadly, none of these come even close to my favorite English euphemism for going to the loo, which is "I am going to turn my bike round!"

CHOUETTE: There are two common French words for "owl": one is *hibou*, which you probably learned at school; the other is *chouette*. Feel free to promptly forget the word *hibou* for the time being. I seemed to hear the word *chouette* a lot when I first came to France but couldn't see why people were mentioning owls all the time. In fact, *chouette* in general usage has nothing whatsoever to do with owls: it means "wonderful," "lovely," brilliant," "kind," "neat," and more. A pretty girl is *chouette*, as is a flashy car or a nice house. If you want to make clear that something is really particularly special, you can combine the word with VACHEMENT and declare whatever it is to be VACHEMENT *chouette*. An extremely kind person, who is not necessarily beautiful, can also be affectionately referred to as *chouette*, too. Incidentally, there is a very old joke about why owls are lucky. The answer, you will be delighted to learn, is because the wife of *un hibou* is *chouette*.

CLOPE: The slang word for a cigarette is *une clope*. Among young people, it is almost universally used: no one says *une cigarette* at all. Young people can often be heard asking one another for a cigarette with the words, "*S'il te plaît. T'as pas une clope?*" and meeting with a high success rate. A light for the cigarette, once they have got one, is *du feu* as in "*T'as du feu?*" As this sort of exchange is between young people, the *tu* form of the verb is used, even though the two people are complete strangers. It is a lesser known fact that while *une clope* means a whole cigarette, *un clope* simply means a cigarette end. So, if you find yourself wanting the whole thing, be careful to use the feminine form.

CON: You have probably been thinking, "What about the rude words, then?" Well, while I have no intention of teaching you all the rude French words, there is one that is really indispensable. What's more, it probably has the widest range of meanings of any French obscenity and thus is the hardest to translate into English. Its only advantage is that it is one of the shortest to write. As an adjective, *con* is simply translated as "bloody stupid," whereas when used as a noun it means something like "stupid git." When someone does something both stupid and annoying, the only thing you can reasonably cry out in your exasperation is *"Quel con!"*—What an ass! There are also a number of longer words, derived from the word *con*, but I'll let you look them up yourselves as they are very rude indeed. My first boss had a favorite phrase which implied, but didn't actually use, the word. When moaning about something daft that someone else had done, he liked to say, *"On est très peu à ne pas l'être"*—There are very few of us who aren't . . . *con*. I was vaguely grateful when he said this because, as he was addressing me, I had to assume that I was included in those who weren't. On good days, I might even have included him!

CONTREPÈTERIE: This is a doubly hard word to deal with. First, you have to understand the meaning of the word. Second, and far harder, you have to understand the point of it all. The first part is easy enough once you know what a spoonerism is, for a *contrepèterie* is roughly the French equivalent thereof. For those unfamiliar with the term, a spoonerism is defined as the accidental transposition of the initial letters of two words in a phrase, a habit for which the Rev. Spooner became famous. For example, he is reputed to have said, "He has just received a blushing crow" instead of "a crushing blow." All spoonerisms are relatively innocent and are often done by accident. *Contrepèteries*, on the other hand, are defined as *"interversion des lettres ou des syllabes d'un ensemble de mots produisant un sens burlesque, souvent obscène.*" They are thus far from innocent and are generally very rude. They are also always done deliberately. We shall turn to Rabelais for a modest example. He wrote *"femme folle à la messe"*—crazy woman at mass—which was intended to make people think of *"femme molle à la fesse"*—woman of soft buttocks. (This was quite racy stuff in Rabelais's day.) My problem is that whenever I am faced with a *contrepèterie*, I just think, "Oh, so what?" I really can't see the point of them at all. They tend mainly to appeal to young men in a state of inebriation. If you don't plan on spending time with such people, I wouldn't bother much with *contrepèteries*.

DODO: Nothing whatever to do with extinct flightless birds. *Dodo* is a familiar, or child's, word for "sleep." Efforts to encourage a child to go to bed are based around sentences like *"Allez! C'est l'heure d'aller au dodo"* or *"On va faire un gros dodo"* and generally meet with as much success as they would in other countries. However, the word also figures in a common expression that sums up the life of a commuter. This is said to consist of *"Métro, boulot, dodo"* and roughly translates as "Commute, work, sleep."

FLOTTE, FLOTTER: That there are lots of slang words for things in French is not surprising. What strikes me as odd is that there are slang words for ordinary, everyday things. There are slang words for books, cars, and even the wind. There is also a common slang word for "water" which is *la flotte*. In its formal sense, *la flotte* means "the fleet" as in a lot of warships all together. There is also a verb *flotter*, which means "to float." The floating sense, as well as the fleet sense, appears to have led to the modern meaning of water. The word is surprisingly common. At mealtimes, you will be asked to *passer la flotte* while thirsty people will throw themselves on *un verre de flotte* and reformed alcoholics drink *que de la flotte*. As well as meaning "to float," *flotter* means "to rain;" young people look out of the window to check whether *il est toujours en train de flotter*, while getting caught in the rain is *j'ai pris la flotte*.

GÉNIAL!: An immensely handy word: *genial* can simply be described as a stronger French version of the word "nice." Everyone uses it, but teenagers especially would be incapable of describing anything favorably without it. You can flatter people with it: *"Vous êtes génial!* You can enthuse about something: *"C'est génial!"* Or just exclaim happily when faced with something special: *"Génial!"* For the opposite of *génial*, please see NUL. Both *génial* and NUL have other, proper meanings that are given in the dictionary.

LAUGHTER WORDS: How many words are there in English for laughing? If you think for a while, you will realize that there aren't that many synonyms for "laughter" or "laugh." You can check, if you like, in a thesaurus. There are words like "chuckle," "chortle," "giggle," or "snigger" but these are low-key affairs and don't really imply loud, memorable laughter. Of course, there are expressions such as "rolling on the floor laughing" or "splitting your sides with laughter," but there really aren't any words that, all by themselves, just mean laughing out loud and enjoying the experience. It must be an indication of some aspect of the French character that they have lots of laughter words. The basic word for "to laugh" is *rire*, which you probably knew. But there are other words, some colloquial, for really laughing out loud, such as *se marrer*, *s'esclafer*, *se bidonner*, *rigoler*, *pouffer*, or *se poiler*. All these words convey a notion of loud, joyous, hearty laughter that English words don't seem to manage. Once you have learned them all, you will realize that each French person tends to have his or her own favorite, which they use all the time.

MERDE!: I have said earlier that you won't find many rude words here. This one is included, not in its usual sense— the one you more than probably know—but because of a more friendly way in which it can be used. For as well as a multipurpose insult that you shout at people when displeased with them, "*Merde!*" can also be used to wish someone luck. It is often thought unlucky to wish someone well for an exam or when they are about to go on stage in a play by saying, "*Bonne chance!*" It has therefore become fairly common to say "*Merde!*" to them instead, a bit like wishing an actor "Break a leg" rather than "Good luck!" Thus, as you say good-bye before whoever it is sets off for their ordeal, you can add, "*Je te dis 'merde!'*" If you are a bit squeamish about actually pronouncing the word *merde* in polite society, you can just leave it out and use a meaning-ful pause instead, saying, "*Pour demain, je te dis . . .*" while nodding meanfully. Using *merde* in this way is quite common: I have just recently heard a journalist on the radio wish luck to the manager of the French rugby team by saying, *"Et . . . merde pour samedi."*

MINCE!: As well as having a fairly comprehensive range of real, serious swear words, the French have a selection of nice or mock swear words which each start with the same letter as the ruder word that they are intended to replace. Thus, instead of saying the favorite French expletive MERDE, many people, apparently in an attempt to sound genteel, will say, *"Mince!"* This not only starts with the same letter as MERDE but has the same number of letters. *Mince* means "thin," which doesn't seem to make it that suitable for a swear word. The major problem seems to be that by saying *mince* you are merely showing everyone that you are trying to sound genteel and thus, in many people's eyes, you end up looking ridiculous.

NUL: We have seen that GÉNIAL is the all-purpose word for expressing enthusiasm and favor, and the opposite is *nul.* While GÉNIAL is invariably pronounced in an enthusiastic manner, with a rising intonation, *nul* is always said in a low, glowering sort of way. As with GÉNIAL, *nul* is more the preserve of teenagers than adults, especially grumpy ones who are grumbling about some minor irritant. *C'est nul!* in an aggrevied tone marks the depths of displeasure. The more upset the teenager, the longer the *u* in the middle of the word. While you are hardly likely to exclaim, *"Wouah!*

C'est nuuul" when visiting a BOULANGERIE on holiday, even if they have sold out of your favorite cakes, you could always while away some time by sidling up to a group of adolescents and counting the number of GÉNIALS and *nul*s that you hear.

OH LA LA!: Everyone knows that French people say "Oh la, la!" when surprised in some way, and I am certainly not going to tell you that they don't. What is interesting is that not all French people seem to say exactly the same thing. Years of attentive listening have convinced me that variations are possible and even commonplace. Everyone uses the same words, of course. It is just the number of words, particularly the *la*s that varies. Friends and colleagues regularly put in an extra *la*, whether for emphasis or because they can't manage to stop in time. However, the resulting three *la*s appear to be considered insufficient, or possibly asymmetric, because it is more common to hear four *la*s rather than three. In either case, the final *la* is noticeably stronger than the preceding ones. This extra stress on the last *la* seems to increase the more *la*s there are. With the basic *oh, la la* the two *la*s are practically indistinguishable, whereas with *oh, la la la la!*, the last *la* is not only stressed but drawn out much longer than the other three. I have a colleague who is the only person I know who, in moments of extreme emotion, will exclaim, *"Oh, la la la la la* la!" the last *la* lasting as long as all the others put together.

OUAIS: Any young English-speaking person generally says

"yeah" instead of "yes." Apart from probable questions of not wanting to conform, they most likely do it because "yeah" is easier to pronounce and requires much less muscle movement than that needed to say "yes" brightly. Not wishing to be outdone by their English-speaking counterparts, French-speaking youth tend to say *ouais* instead of *oui* for pretty much the same reasons. Saying *ouais*, like saying "yeah," just involves letting your mouth fall open without any sideways effort at all, while making a sound pretty much like grunting. Saying *oui*, on the other hand, makes you draw the sides of your mouth apart in a tiring sort of rictus. Also, people in general tend to show skepticism at an idea by replying, "*Mmmouais*." This starts off with a sort of humming through closed lips followed up by an elided *ouais*. In the Lucky Luke cowboy comic books, in order to imitate real cowboys who say, "Yep!" Lucky Luke says, "*Ouap*."

POTE: We have seen that *un* COPAIN is a slang word for "a friend." There is a similar word, *un pote*, which, while it also means "a friend," implies somehow that it is a particularly close friend, one of the good ones. By saying of someone *c'est un pote*, you make it clear that he is someone that you appreciate and can rely on. If you want to show that he is extra special, you will refer to him as *un bon pote*. A bloke walking into a bar to find his mates already there will greet them collectively with the words, "*Salut, les potes!*" This notion of special friendship led to the word being adopted in a campaign against racism where support for immigrants was based on the slogan *"Touche pas à mon pote!"*—Hands off my mate!—set out on a badge shaped like the palm of a hand.

Punaise/purée: As we have seen, people use the word MINCE as a substitute for MERDE. The list of French swear words also includes the far stronger and much less pleasant word (which you should on no account use) *putain*. This word when used to describe someone means "whore" or "slut" but it can also be used as a sign of exasperation or anger when it more commonly becomes *"Oh! Putain!"* However, as this is quite strong, there are a couple of parallel words that sound vaguely similar and can be used instead in much the same way as some people exclaim, "Oh! Sugar!" instead of "Oh shit!" These are *"Punaise!"* which used in other circumstances means "thumbtack" or a variety of beetle, and *"Purée!"* which means "mashed potato." Clearly, anyone shouting "Thumbtack!" or, worse, "Mashed potato!" at moments of extreme emotion is someone to be treated with suspicion.

Quoi . . . ?: In English, young people shower their sentences with filler words such as "like" and "I mean," not to mention "you know." In France, the single word without which young people would go into spasm each time they tried to say anything is *quoi*. This literally means "what" but is generally tacked on the end of a more or less coherent sentence to show that the speaker has gotten to the end of it, such as it is, and that it's probably your turn for a go

now. A variant on the theme is to finish with the words
voilà, quoi. This means, "That's all that I have to say on the
matter so there is no point in hoping for any more." The
word *voilà* is spoken on a rising tone, while the *quoi* finishes
on a falling one. School teachers love to ask their pupils
to make a brief presentation to the class without ending it
with *bien, voilà, quoi.* Very few of them manage it.

Sympa: One of the first English words that foreign students
learn is "nice." As soon as they have learned it, they can
make up a whole range of simple sentences in which they
describe things that they like as "nice" and things that they
don't like as "not nice." You will be pleased to learn that
there is a French word that can be used as widely as "nice"
to describe things that you like. The word is *sympathique*,
but it is more commonly abbreviated to *sympa.* Someone
you like or who has been kind to you would earn, "*Il est
sympa*" or even "*Il est très sympa.*" If someone does something nice, you could thank him or her not with a simple
merci or even *merci beaucoup* but by saying, "*Merci, c'est
sympa.*" It can be used ironically when someone makes you
do something that you didn't want to: *C'est sympa!* or even,
if a group of blokes are involved, *Sympa, les mecs!* As with
"not nice" you can define a lot of things, or people, or even
places, as being *pas sympa* or *pas très sympa.* An unfriendly
person could be described with *il n'est pas très sympa* or, if
he was really unpleasant, *il n'est pas sympa du tout.* Once
you have started using *sympa*, you will wonder how you
managed without it.

TA GUEULE!: This phrase is almost indispensable either if you want a quiet life or if you are planning on having a row with someone, for it means "Shut up!" *Gueule* literally means "the muzzle of an animal," but it has come to mean "a person's face." Indeed, if you don't like the look of someone you would say that *"il a une sale gueule"* or *"je n'aime pas sa gueule."* *Ta gueule* is used exactly like "shut up" so I don't need to give you any examples. However, the fact that the expression is constructed in the *tu* form does not mean that, should you find yourself having a violent argument with a stranger, or your boss, you should try and construct it in the *vous* form. Saying *votre gueule* to an unpleasant stranger is unimaginably absurd! In any case, if you have reached the point where you are forced to say *ta gueule* to a stranger, you are past worrying about his sensibilities. There are, however, those who, when faced with several noisy individuals, typically children, tend to shout *vos gueules* to them all rather than *ta gueule* individually. By the way, a slightly more polite way of encouraging someone to cease talking is to say, *"Tais-toi."* This can be modified to *taisez-vous* as the need arises.

TRUC: In English we have a thingy or a whatsit or the like to define an object that we can't be bothered to name correctly, or don't actually know the name of. In French there are two vital words to learn as soon as possible in order to have any chance of understanding what people are talking about. They are *un truc* and *un machin*, both of which mean "a thing." Asking for something in a shop when you don't know what it is really called becomes so much easier when you can say that you are looking for *un truc qui fait . . .* , going on to explain what it does, possibly waving your hands about to help make yourself understood. *Truc* can also be used for the solution to a problem or a cunning way of dealing with something. You would boast about this by saying, *"J'ai trouvé le truc!"* The word *machin* can even be used for a person who you don't know, or can't be bothered to name, though this is exceedingly uncomplimentary. There are compound words that mean the same thing as *truc* but are more entertaining, such as *machin-chouette* or even *un machin-truc* when you really have *no idea* what else to call it.

VACHEMENT: On reading this you probably deduced that it had something to do with cows. Think again. *Vachement* is a word that means "amazingly" or "extremely" and is the slang word that is used in place of proper words such as *extrêmement* or *particulièrement*. The majority of young people, and quite a few of the older ones, would be hard put to have a conversation without using this word. Whether you are describing how pretty the girl was—*"Elle était vachement jolie"*—or how fast the bloke on the motorbike was going—*"Il allait vachement vite"*—or how really expensive it was—*"C'était vachement cher"*—you really can't do without it. Despite appearances, though, it really has nothing to do with cows whatsoever.

VERLAN: This is the French form of back slang—a way of creating new slang words by reversing the order of the syllables of an existing word. The word for "backward" is *à l'envers*. If you take *à l'envers* and apply the principal of back slang to it, you end up with *verlan*. *Verlan* is principally used by young people in the poorer suburbs of Paris, but its use is so widespread that practically all young people use a word now and again, sometimes unknowingly. A common example is MEUF instead of *femme* as we have seen under FILLE, but all sorts of common words have their *verlan* equivalent, to the bemusement of many parents. When feeling upset or uptight, people used to be *énervé*; now, they are *vénère*. You no longer refer to your mother as *ma mère* but as *ma rem* and describe tedious people not as *lourd* but as *re-lou*. I even know of one person whose dog—*le chien*—is referred to as *le ienche*.

Relations (Family and Others)

It is sad to think that up to this point you have probably been walking into French shops in silence. All that is soon to change! This section deals with meeting and greeting people and includes a few words to do with people whom you know rather better than others. A beginner's guide to kissing people on the cheeks is followed by the real reason why certain professional people attach plastic bags to trees.

You will also find a selection of words relating to members of the family, from very young to quite old.

Greetings *and* Expressions

Au plaisir!: There is an expression *au plaisir de vous revoir* which the dictionary defines as being a friendly salutation when taking your leave. It roughly translates as "looking forward to seeing you again," and can be used, for example, when saying good-bye politely to someone whom you have just met. Alternatively, a salesperson, or someone who has been providing some kind of service to a customer, may use it after saying good-bye. Hearing the whole expression is generally quite rare. You are much more likely to hear someone just say, *"Au plaisir!"* as an alternative to *au revoir*. However, there is a slight problem with this expression because, to put it bluntly, saying *au plaisir* is considered a bit common by certain people. My esteemed family-in-law has unfortunately trained me to believe that several words in these pages are considered common, though I think that this one is viewed by them as being one of the worst. Rather than take their word for it, you should perhaps listen for this and other expressions and judge for yourself.

BCBG: Four letters which sum up an entire lifestyle. They stand for *bon chic, bon genre*, which roughly means "someone who dresses tastefully and comes from a good family." Calling someone *BCBG* conveys the fact that they not only look nice, but they may be supposed to buy quality, fashionable clothes that will probably suit them. If that wasn't enough, such people, given that they come from a good family, can confidently be expected to behave "nicely." People will describe someone to you by saying, "*Elle est très BCBG,*" and everyone will know what to expect. A style of clothes could be described as *un look BCBG*.

The late comedian Jacques Villeret declared that the letters in fact stood for *beau cul, belle gueule*, which means "nice butt and a nice face."

BON APPÉTIT!: This is an expression that is used by practically everyone in France with the notable exception of my family-in-law who resolutely maintains that it is common. Of course, if you are at a meal where someone says it to you, it is only polite to say it back. The problem is, being English, you often get asked by French people when sitting down for a meal how you say *bon appétit* in English. Things start to go downhill from that point because you are forced to reply that there is no real expression that corresponds to the spirit of *bon appétit* and have to suggest that they should say something long-winded like "I hope you enjoy your meal." Once you have said this, you run the risk of someone unkindly pointing out that of course there is no need for such an expression in England because

English food is so bad that no one can be expected to enjoy a meal there. It is wise at this point to distract whomever it is by getting the subject off food and on to sex as soon as possible, assuming that circumstances permit it, to avoid things degenerating rapidly.

BONNE CONTINUATION: I am fairly sure that I can translate all the words in this book into English except this one. I know what it means, and when it is used, but have really no idea of its English equivalent. *Bonne continuation* is like *bon courage* in that it is a throwaway, friendly sort of thing that you say to someone at the end of a conversation, however brief. Waiters, for example, say it when they have brought a new dish to the table. Also, people who have been talking to you while you are doing something, and who leave you to get on with it, say it as they go away. It basically means, "I hope that you carry on enjoying whatever it is that you are currently doing, and preferably enjoying it even more than you did before we started talking." In the case of a meal, the waiter wants you to carry on enjoying your food and generally having a good time. In the case of some other activity, it means a cross between "carry on," "keep up the good work," and "have a nice day." I really can't be more specific than that.

BON . . . , BONNE . . . : Following on from the previous paragraph, you can make a friendly expression to suit pretty much any occasion simply by starting it with *bon . . .* or *bonne . . .* You can wish someone a nice day with *bonne* *journée*, a safe journey by saying *bonne route*, or *bonne retour* for a good trip back. But there is no real limit to this kind of thing: someone announcing that they are going to put their washing in can be encouraged with a friendly *bonne lessive*, or you can even show support for someone's tidying up by saying, *"Bon rangement"* without sounding in the least silly.

BONJOUR, M'SSIEURS, DAMES: Just listen the next time you go into any kind of bar or small shop in France, and you will hear people using the all-purpose, universal salutation *"Bonjour, messieurs, dames"* as they walk in. Practically everybody says it. It is an abbreviated form of *bonjour, messieurs, mesdames*—which should, in fact, more correctly be *bonjour, mesdames, bonjour, messieurs*—a complete, and formal, greeting that practically no one ever uses. Translated into English it sounds like an emcee walking onto a stage and greeting the audience by saying, "Good morning, ladies and gentlemen." In French it just passes for a collective "hello." The only essential thing is that there must be two or more people present, or at least, a probability that at least two people are going to be there when you open the door and walk in. The *bonjour* part can even be dropped, leaving a shortened greeting—*messieurs, dames*—which, in extreme circumstances, can be pared away to leave just *m'sieurs, dames*. The reply to the universal salutation is, however, different. You cannot reply to a *bonjour, messieurs, dames* with your own *bonjour, messieurs, dames*: it just doesn't work. It would be illogical and would sound daft because, while whoever said it first had been greeting several people at once, you would only be greeting the latest, single person who said it to you. You should therefore limit your reply to a simple *bonjour* or, if you are feeling formal, use a more specific *bonjour, monsieur* or *bonjour, madame* according to circumstance.

PARDON: In English, if you haven't heard what someone has said and want him or her to repeat it, you have several possibilities. You can choose between several words including *sorry?, what?, pardon?*, or simply *eh?* The French have a similar choice of words. Probably the most formal is *"Pardon?"* which, if you want to really go over the top, can be extended to *"Pardon? Pouvez-vous répéter?"* Or even, if you really want to make an issue of it, you can say, *"Je vous demande pardon."* But of course, in real life, no one says that. What they do say the most often is *"Comment?"* the tone and the accent varying to suit the situation. Further down the scale comes *"Quoi?"* which roughly corresponds to the English "What?" And then, near the bottom of the scale is a sound, rather than a word, which is spelled "Hein?" This can only really be pronounced properly if you curl your upper lip and wrinkle your nose. This is the French version of "Eh?" or "Huh?" Finally, you can still occasionally encounter charming elderly people of the old school who, instead of saying the formal *"Pardon?"* use the very polite, and extremely old-fashioned, *"Plaît-il?"* If you want to stand out from the crowd next time you are in France, try saying *"Plaît-il?"* instead of *"Pardon?"*

Re-: If you have ever felt that a French person may have growled at you for no apparent reason, this may provide the explanation. When you meet someone for the first time on a given day, whether it is in the office or outside, you of course say *bonjour*. But what happens if you bump into him or her again in the course of the same day? Typically what happens is that one person will say *bonjour* again, then remember that you have already seen each other that day and correct his greeting to *re-bonjour* where the *re* part just means "again." This is all very well and good. What is disturbing are the people who, instead of saying *re-bonjour*, drop the key part of the greeting and just say *re-*. This sounds like a growly sort of "Rruh!" Thus, through no fault of your own, you can find yourself growled at, though at least now you know why.

Salut: The Italian greeting *ciao* has always struck me as incredibly handy because you can use it both when you meet someone and when you take your leave from them. To the best of my knowledge, there is no comparable hello/good-bye word in English. The French, however, can claim one up on the English because they have got one of their own. It is *salut*. It is far less formal than *bonjour* and is commonly used between friends who don't need to stand on ceremony. A brief survey in my office revealed that six out of seven colleagues greeted me by just saying, "*Salut!*" Most young people would be hard put to greet their contempories without using it. You can combine *salut* with other words that we will discover later to give greetings such as "*Salut, les* MECS!" or "*Salut, les* COPAINS!" Incidentally, the French equivalent of the Salvation Army is "*L'Armée du Salut.*" This does not mean the greetings army, as *salut* in this context means "salvation."

Sex, *or* as Close as We Are Going to Come to It

BAISER: If you thought that this was the French for "to kiss," think again. I am sure that I am not the only one to have been taught at school that this was what it meant, happily writing something like "*Le monsieur baise sa femme*" in my French I exam. Unfortunately, as a verb *baiser* in fact means "to screw," or whatever vulgar term you prefer for the act of procreation. It thus implies a far greater degree of intimacy than just kissing. I wonder if whoever corrected my French I test knew this. Perhaps it explains my low grade? The proper, current word for "to kiss" is *embrasser*. However, when used as a noun, *un baiser* does indeed mean "a kiss"; girls are heard to ask, "*Donne-moi un baiser*" of their boyfriends without any intention of this leading to any unseemly activity. Slightly lower down the intimacy scale comes *un bisou*, which means a brief or small kiss along the lines of a peck on the cheek. You can also use terms like *bons baisers* or *gros bisous* to finish a letter where, in English you would put "love and kisses."

BAISE-EN-VILLE: Having learned all about the verb BAISER, you are now in a position to appreciate this term. A *baise-en-ville* literally means "having it off in town" and the phrase in French refers to a small bag, about the size of a carry-all, that is intended to be able to contain the essential necessities that you are presumed to need for an illicit rendezvous. Such a meeting generally, or so I am told, takes place in the early evening and thus is known as *un cinq à sept*. However, I had a colleague who carried one of those small leather bags with a strap, about the size of a book, and which were all the rage in France a few years ago. He resolutely referred to this bag as his *baise-en-ville* even though it contained nothing more exotic than his keys, cigarettes, and a pack of tissues.

BISE: *La bise* is the act of kissing someone on both cheeks, generally twice but sometimes four times, and, even more rarely, three times. Mastering it is more difficult than it looks. As in kissing someone's hand, where you don't actually kiss it, kissing someone's cheek involves putting your cheek to hers and making a kissing sound rather than actually smacking your lips into her cheek. Clearly, two people can't kiss each other's cheeks at the same time as the angles don't work. Practice it in the privacy of your own homes before letting yourself loose on your first victim, bearing in mind that it is vitally important to keep your lips away from theirs. Once you have mastered the act of kissing, you have to decide what sort of kisser you are going to be. There are people who kiss twice, some who kiss three times, and the rest who kiss four times. There are also self-claimed experts who will talk at length on what sort of person will kiss a given number of times, and there are even people who try to draw parallels between particular regions of France and the number of kisses given. Such people will even quote particular villages deep in rural France (of which there is an awful lot) where all the inhabitants give a single *bise*. Experience has taught me to be extremely skeptical of all this. As far as I can see, you can never tell what sort of person you may be confronted with. Finally, there are even differences in the sounds people make during *la bise*. These can range from near silence to extraordinarily loud smacking sounds made from the opposite corner of one's mouth to the other person's cheek.

If you decide that you are a two-kiss person everything is fine as long as you are faced with fellow two-kiss people. However, if you encounter a four-kiss person, for example at a friend's house, things tend to go to pieces. You will do your two kisses to your fellow guest and then start to pull away, believing that the job is done. She, on the other hand, will only be halfway through her planned four-kiss routine and will be leaning forward for the third kiss. Noting to your horror that she hasn't pulled away but is going for a third kiss, you will rapidly lean back toward her to accept the third one. Either you will bump noses at this point, or the other person, having by then realized that you were only going to do two kisses, has started to pull away, too, cutting short her own program. In that case, you may well end up chasing her backward trying desperately to finish the four kisses that you have now belatedly set about doing. If there is a group of people meeting or saying good-bye who have different kissing habits, you may hear someone doing four kisses with other members of the group and note the fact accordingly. Unfortunately, they may have already heard you just doing your two kisses and may thus have decided to only do two to you when your turn comes around, while you have decided to give them four. Thus the four-kiss person will be about to do two kisses, while you, trying to fit in with them, will be about to change and do four. Chaos generally ensues. Some helpful people announce in advance what sort of kisser they are: "*Moi, c'est quatre*"—I do four—they say, and you act accordingly. It has been suggested that some kind of sign or hand signal be adopted in order to show in advance what kind of kisser you are. This strikes me as an excellent idea but I am not sure who to approach to try and get it accepted. L'Académie Française perhaps?

CALIN: When a small child is upset, or in need of comfort or reassurance, he or she will generally go to a parent or close friend and ask, "*Tu me fais un calin?*" *Un calin* is a hug or a cuddle. Similarly, when people show kittens, puppies, or other small fury animals to small children they will urge the child to stroke it by saying, "*Tu lui fais des calins?*" The term can also be used as an adjective. For example, a parent will be heard saying of their child, "*Il est très calin,*" when they mean that the child is a bit delicate and likes to be hugged and made a fuss of occasionally.

And who among us doesn't? There are, yet again, those who say that *calin* is only used by people in the lower social orders. In its extreme sense, the term can refer to something far more sexual in nature, the sort of thing that generally only occurs between consenting adults. I discovered this when a large and singularly unattractive female colleague explained her late arrival at work that morning by the fact that her husband *"a voulu faire un gros calin"* before leaving for the office. My colleagues and I were appalled and unanimously felt that this could best be described as "too much information."

COPAIN, COPINE: When I first spent time in France I was lucky enough to do so in the company of a delightful young lady who, when I referred to her in English, I was proud to call "my girlfriend." But how should I refer to her in French? It seemed, at the time, that I had the choice between the somewhat old-fashioned *ma petite amie* and the more modern *ma copine*. *Ma petite amie* when pronounced in my charming English accent invariably made people smile so I thought I'd go for *ma copine*. In general, *une copine* is the slang term for a female friend, a male friend being *un copain*. Changing to *ma* or *mon* alters the meaning from just "a friend" to "girlfriend" or "boyfriend." Thus introducing someone as *un copain* is quite different from saying, *"Je vous présente mon copain."* There are girls who prefer to make things quite clear and refer to male friends as *un copain* while their boyfriend is known as *mon petit copain* even if he is quite tall. Later on, when you reach the age of live-in partners, the terms *copain/copine* no longer seem suitable. People seem to refer to such partners simply as *mon ami* or *mon amie*, only the silent *e* indicating the sex.

FÊTE, BOUM, SOIRÉE, TEUF: One of the principal signs of impending old age in France typically occurs shortly after your thirtieth birthday and centers on that terrible moment when you realize that you no longer know how to define a party. A party, a word that I use for want of a better one to define a social evening where several adolescents or young people gather in the presence of loud music and alcohol, is a tricky thing to describe in French. Each generation has had its own word for the thing. No sooner have you learned the word than it is out of date. As far as I can see, those who are now grandparents called such an event *une soirée*—or "evening." Those who are parents used to go to *une boum*. This is witnessed by a film from the early eighties (starring the incomparable Sophie Marceau) called *La Boum*. Those who are younger go to *une fête* while those who are younger still use the back slang (VERLAN) version of the word *fête*, which is *teuf*. Don't bother trying to learn any of these—they are doubtless already out of date. If you want to ask a young person if they are going to such an event, you will just have to use a neutral expression like, "*Est-ce que vous sortez ce soir?*" and hope that you will recognize the word used in reply.

MARQUES D'AFFECTION: The English are remarkably restrained when it comes to words of endearments—they call loved ones things like "sweetie, dear, honey," etc. but nothing really surprising. The French version of endearments runs the whole gamut from animal to vegetable. Unfortunately, I can't think of a mineral one. Most of the odder ones, it must be said, are addressed to small children. Let's start with things animal: it is quite common to hear mothers address their small children as *ma puce* without anyone batting an eyelid. I have always found this odd, as *puce* means "flea." Moving up the scale, children can also be referred to as *ma caille* which means "quail" or sometimes *ma poulette*, or "chicken." Am I the only one to find nothing endearing in either a flea or a quail? As to things vegetable, many loving mothers call their small offspring *mon chou* which sounds quite sweet until you remember that *chou* means "cabbage." (Okay, I admit that *chou* is actually used in its alternative sense of "puff pastry" in this context, but even that isn't very flattering.) Other common terms are *mon canard*, or "my duck," and *mon sucre d'orge*, which means "my barley sugar."

SAC EN PLASTIQUE: This, you won't be surprised to learn, is French for a "plastic bag." Some people abbreviate it to *un sac plastique*, but it is probably better to stick to the whole thing. If you go south and find yourself beyond the Garonne river, you will have to learn to ask for *une poche* instead of *un sac en plastique*, otherwise you won't get one. However, the real point of this paragraph is to explain what conclusion to draw if you find yourself driving through a forest in the Paris area and spot a plastic bag tied to a tree by the roadside. Assuming it has been tied, and not simply blown there, such a bag means that there is a lady of the night who is waiting for customers in a clearing immediately adjacent to the tree with the bag. Should you desire to avail yourself of her services (or possibly of *his* services, despite the fact that you won't necessarily be able to spot this at first glance) you should also be aware that, if she is waiting in a van, the fact that the curtains are open means that she is available for business. Drawn curtains mean that she is currently engaged and you should come back later. And to think that last time you drove through a French forest, you thought it was just a bag in a tree!

Family *Members,* Young and Old

ARHEU: If you are going to have anything to do with small babies in France, or speak to anyone who has one, this is a key word, or rather sound, to learn. For French babies do not gurgle and they certainly don't imitate their British cousins by going "goo." French babies say, *"Arheu, arheu."* So does anyone who talks to a baby. Unfortunately, this is a fiendishly difficult sound to make for English speakers who can't roll their *r*'s. As it is forbidden by statute to come face to face with a French baby and not make the sound, you have the choice between avoiding babies altogether, or having a go at saying it and sounding painfully foreign. It is probably best to have a go anyway, while comforting yourself with the thought that at least the baby probably won't notice how bad your accent is.

LE PETIT, LA PETITE: People have children in France. No surprises so far. What is different is the way that members of some families seem to refer to their children. In English, people with several children may introduce them to visitors by saying, "This is my eldest, George, and this is our youngest, Fiona." In France, terms corresponding to "the oldest" and "the youngest" are also used, but these terms take on such importance that they end up becoming used instead of the children's actual names. The youngest child of three or more, and occasionally the younger of two, will be known as *le petit* or *la petite*, according to sex. With time, this manages to become the name of the child in the eyes of at least his or her parents. Thus, instead of asking where the youngest child has got to, one parent will ask the other, "*T'as vu la petite?*" and not "*T'as vu Martine?*" It is not clear what they write on labels for Christmas presents. If the children are close in age or in size, it can be confusing for third parties who can't readily spot which one is *la petite*. This naming system applies at least until the child in question reaches twelve, and often beyond. Where there are three or more children, the eldest may be known as *la grande* or *le grand*. The one in the middle is probably the only one to be called by his real name.

PÉPÉ, MÉMÉ, PAPY, MAMIE, ETC.: You may have been troubled by the question as to how the French refer to their grandparents. The correct individual words for *les grand-parents* are *grandpère* and *grandmère*. While these are the *correct* terms for grandparents, there are other words that you should know, but not necessarily use. For, as with so many things, the choice of word is a function of certain social conditions. If you are from a titled family, or try to pretend that you are, you may refer to your elders as *bonne-maman* and *bon-papa*. If, however, you descend below the level of *grandpère et grandmère,* you will know your parents' parents as *papy et mamie*. And why not? Calling them *Pépé et Mémé*, on the other hand, starts to get worrying, while those who get presents signed "*Pépère et Mémère*" will be unlikely to be invited to our house. However, the word *pépère*, given that it conjures up images of portly, placid old men, can be used as an adjective meaning "peaceful or easygoing" and can be used, for example, to describe an untaxing job or a friendly old dog.

PIPI, CACA: We have seen that the word ARHEU is vitally useful if you ever have dealings with French babies. But what happens if you have to talk to small French children? If you spend any length of time with them, it is likely at some point that the question of bodily functions will arise. But which words should you use? There are two principal words in common usage, one for each function. These are *pipi* and *caca*. A simple rule will suffice before we move on to the next subject: *pipi* is okay; *caca* quite definitely isn't.

$\mathscr{D}$AY-TO-DAY LIFE

These are simply words that you will come across in newspa-pers, magazines, or when watching the news.

Mind you, my favorite is the one about suppositories, and you won't find them mentioned often on the news.

Buying a bed in France will be revealed as being tougher than you thought, while tuning a musical instrument turns out to be a lot easier.

ARME BLANCHE: This is one of the French expressions where, despite the fact that you can understand each of the two words that make it up, you can't begin to guess what it actually means. *Arme blanche* means literally "white weapon" but this is no help at all because, of course, the thing in question is not actually white at all, though it is in fact a weapon. *Une arme blanche* is the generally used term for a knife, more specifically the sort of knife used for stabbing people in a fight rather than one used in a kitchen, even though these are often one and the same. It is a common term in news reports where assorted thugs are described as fighting or attacking each other *à l'arme blanche*. The term *blanche* apparently refers to the fact that a knife is made of steel, and thus could be conceivably viewed as white when opposed to the bronze used in other types of weapon such as handguns.

BIC: Each country seems to choose particular brand names to turn into common words for everyday objects. English speakers have opted for Hoover and Thermos when talking about a vacuum cleaner or an insulated mug, for example. In the U.K., Mr. Biro, the inventor of the ballpoint pen, has also been thus immortalized. Unfortunately, calling for *un biro* in France will not inspire anyone to lend you their ballpoint pen. If you want a loan of such an implement, you will have to ask, "*Pouvez-vous me prêter un bic, s'il vous plaît?*" even though the pen that you will be lent will more likely have come from Japan than from Baron Bich's factories in France. Since their success in producing simple ballpoint pens, the Bic company has branched out into making disposable lighters and even surfboards, though neither of these products seem to be referred to as "Bics."

BIS: An interesting little word that can be used in two different ways. The first place that you will most likely spot it is on house numbers. If a new house is built between number 24 and number 26, it will not be known as 24a in France, but will rejoice in the name of 24*bis*. *Bis* (pronounced "beece" and not "biz") means "doubling up," or "doing again." If another house is put up between 24*bis* and number 26, it will be known as 24*ter*. *Bis* is also the word that you shout out at French concerts where, ironically enough had you been in England, you would have shouted "encore." It is cried to encourage the musician to repeat the bit he has just sung, rather than to encourage him to come back and do something extra. From the musician's point of view, he has been *bissé* by his enthusiastic audience.

CHIFFRES: French numbers are tricky. The complex French counting system is explained under NUMÉROS DE TELEPHONE later on. But, as well as counting difficulties, there are also complicated traps with numbers that don't take an *s* in their plural forms when you could reasonably think that they should. For while *cinq cents* and *cinq millions* each have an *s* at the end, the word for "thousand"—*mille*—is known as INVARIABLE and thus doesn't take an *s* even when you write *dix mille*. *Cent* is, however, even trickier than *mille* because while *cinq cents* has an *s*, as soon as you add any words after the *cent* it loses its *s*. Thus, you write *cinq cent trente* or *six cent quarante trois* without an *s* on the end of *cent*. Finally, there is the question of numbers with hyphens. Strictly, when you write the numbers between sixty and ninety-nine, you should scatter hyphens about the place. Thus, you should write *soixante-dix* or *quatre-vingt-douze* and not *soixante dix* or *quatre vingt douze*, even though practically no one does so anymore. If, by any chance, you are still following, and haven't already moved on to the next entry, *vingt* in numbers like *quatre-vingts* behaves like *cent* in that it only takes a final s when there are no other words afterward.

COUP DE COEUR: You can't go into a record shop, a book-shop, or a restaurant without a fair chance of seeing this. In any review of books, records, or wine, one of them will be selected as being someone's *coup de coeur* or particular favorite. A bookshelf containing the latest bestsellers will include a handwritten note by one of the members of the bookshop's staff setting out the reasons why a particular book had been especially enjoyed. This will be labeled as "*notre coup de coeur*." Similarly, in restaurants that put up a board with a chalked-up list of dishes of the day, they will also suggest the wine of the month, which is invariably called their "*coup de coeur*." The use of the term *coup de coeur* rather than something neutral like *le vin du mois* sets out to make you believe that someone really has tried it and liked it so much that they honestly feel that your life will be improved by drinking it, too. In fact, they are really doing you a favor by mentioning it.

DÉGRIFFÉ: I had great difficulty understanding this word, mainly because I didn't know what *griffé* was. I only knew the first sense of the word *griffe*, which is "claw," *griffé* thus meaning "clawed." There is, however, another equally common meaning of *une griffe* which is "a designer label, mark, or signature." This is what the perfume brand Ma griffe is referring to and not, as I had originally supposed, to someone's claw. Designer label clothes are thus referred to as *griffés*. When such clothes are sold off at the end of a season in a discount saleroom, the designer labels are ripped out. The clothes are thus *dégriffés* or unbranded, end-of-the-line reductions. You thus hear women showing off their new dress or coat, boasting about how cheaply they bought it as it was *dégriffé*.

DIX-HUIT/18: What do you do in the event of an emergency in France? Unlike in the U.K. and the U.S., where there is one phone number to dial whatever situation you find yourself in, in France, of course, things are different. If you want the police, it is simple: you just dial 17. However, if you are faced with any kind of accident or life-threatening incident, then you call the fire brigade or *les pompiers* by dialing 18. "Ah," I hear you say, "but what do I dial if I want an ambulance?" Simple: you call the fire brigade. If it is a real emergency, a fire, a road traffic accident or whatever, you are expected to deal with the *pompiers*. This is particularly true in the Paris area. None of the Parisians I know thinks it is in any way odd to summon the fire brigade for someone who has had a car crash or a heart attack in the street. If there really is a fire, a fire engine turns up when you dial 18. If however, it is a medical problem, you get the SAMU, *Le Service d'Aide Médicale Urgente.* This is a fire-engine-red van filled with *pompiers* who are also paramedics. People generally inaccurately refer to the emergency vehicle itself as a SAMU. This is very annoying for the blokes inside who believe that they are driving a SMUR—*Service Mobile d'Urgence et de Réanimation.* Calling an ambulance, which you do by dialing 15, is for minor dramas when there is more time available. Indeed, if you call an ambulance for a big emergency, they will generally route you through to the *pompiers.* By the way, while the French traditionally dislike their police and find them stupid, they absolutely adore their firemen.

DOIGTS: The French are surprisingly organized when it comes to naming their fingers. Each French finger has its own name, rather than a vague description as in English where they are called "the ring finger" or "the middle finger." In French starting from the one nearest the thumb, which is just called *la pouce*, you have *l'index*; *le majeur*—middle/biggest finger; *l'annulaire*—ring finger; and, last but not least, *l'auriculaire*—little finger. The word *auriculaire* comes from the Latin word for "ear" because the finger in question is the only one that is small enough to stick in your ear! For the French are great ones for scratching an itchy ear. It seems absurd to generalize about a nation when it relates to something as peculiar as ear scratching, but I am forced to do so: French men have a particular way of scratching their ears. I imagine that you have never been struck by the way an Englishman scratches an itch in his ear. It is hardly the sort of thing you notice. Any Englishman faced with an itch would, I'm sure, try to deal with it as discreetly as possible, perhaps using the tip of an index finger. In France things are far more spectacular. I have observed loads of men on trains or buses, or passing the time in their car at a traffic light, who insert the tip of their *auriculaire* as far as it will go in the ear, while keeping the other fingers clenched and the elbow well out to the side. Then, once the little finger is in place, they will shake it with surprising violence both round and round and in and out for some seconds. Then, with an expression of relief and contentment, the finger is removed. It is the violence and duration of the operation that make it so astonishing!

ÉCOUTEZ!: If you want to be sure of hearing this word, ask a prominent figure a question. The more important the person, the more likely he will begin his reply with "*Écoutez!*" The word literally means "Listen!" but is used as a sort of warming-up moment where the person replying is still marshaling his thoughts, but doesn't want anyone else to start talking. It also serves to make sure that the other person is paying attention and is ready for whatever momentous thing is about to be said. It is very rare indeed to see a politician being interviewed on the TV who doesn't answer at least one question with the word. It sometimes appears that the more annoying the politician finds the question, the more he is likely to start with "*Écoutez!*" in a firm tone. Used very aggressively, it can almost mean "Now you just listen to me . . ." If you know the person well and say *tu* to him or her, you will say "*Écoute!*" instead of "*Écoutez!*" Some people, notably my boss, use this as a means of showing that he is on familiar terms with someone important. When telling me about a conversation that he has had with some such person, he will say something like, "So I said to him, '*Écoute, Pierre . . .*' " from which it is clear that he is on intimate terms with whoever it is. Unfortunately for him, this fails to impress me in the slightest.

ELECTIONS: If you follow French presidential elections, even if you can't vote in them, you are going to need to learn a few words. First of all, they are generally carried out in two stages: an elimination round, known as *le premier tour*, and a final contest between the two candidates who received the most votes in the first round and known, unsurprisingly, as *le second tour*. The actual voting procedure is complex. You have to go to your local polling station, which is often the one at the local *mairie*, clutching your *carte électorale* or your identity card. Scrupulous checks of the electoral roll are then made before you are allowed to go into *l'isoloir*, a voting booth which has a curtain extending down to waist height. On the way to *l'isoloir* you have to pick up at least two voting slips which each bear the name of a candidate because voting is carried out by putting a preprinted slip of paper in the voting envelope rather than marking a cross against a name on a list. You are not allowed to take just one slip because this would allow an observer to know who you have voted for. This is taken very seriously and leads to a huge wastage of voting slips, some people picking up one for each of the candidates who, in the first round, can be quite numerous. Having put your voting slip in the envelope, you then leave the booth and head for the ballot box where your name is checked again. Once all is well, the man will pull a lever to open the slot on the top of the bow, watch carefully while you post in your vote, and then declare loudly, "*A voté!*" whereupon a mark is made against your name. Voting closes at eight P.M. at which point all the TV channels announce the winner on the basis of detailed exit polls which have been carried out throughout the day.

EXCLUSION: An all-purpose word that concerns the difficult relationship between the "haves" and the "have nots" in France. France has its share of homeless people, drug addicts, and immigrants, any one of whose future is uncertain. Whenever newspapers refer to the problems of such unfortunates, the word *l'exclusion* is generally used to cover their common difficulties. Such difficulties are generally related to the fact that the better-off people, those who have jobs, a home, and a future, not only don't do anything active to improve the unlucky ones' lot, they pretend that they don't exist. The fact of being ignored and rejected by society is summed up by the word *l'exclusion*. Politicians make long and impassioned speeches urging action *contre l'exclusion*, while charities raise money so as to be able to *se battre contre l'exclusion*, but nothing much seems to change. The homeless, the unemployed, and the other "have nots" are generally referred to as *les exclus*. Bringing the *exclus* back into society, by giving them a job or a home, is defined as *reinsertion*.

FNAC: Everyone goes to *la fnac*. *La fnac*—pronounced *phnack*—is a chain of multimedia shops. If you want to buy a CD, a book, a BD, or any sort of electronic gadget, you generally start at *la fnac*. The large modern shops, easily identifiable by their friendly, lower-case white letters, are in every shopping center. When someone mentions that he is looking for a book to buy, he will very rarely say that he will go and have a look in his local *librairie* or bookshop, but will think first of all of *la fnac*. The shops are popular because they carry consumer surveys and publish useful, free reports setting out the various advantages and disadvantages of the various wares on sale. It is also a handy place to buy tickets for exhibitions and concerts. I doubt whether one French person in ten has any idea where the name "fnac" comes from, though I have never heard anyone comment on what an odd-sounding thing it is. It is, in fact, an acronym for *Fédération Nationale d'Achats pour Cadres* or *National Federation for Management Purchasing*. Once the chain started to become famous, it changed its name, in a spirit of democratization, to *Fédération Nationale d'Achats*, dispensing with the management bit.

HLM: Another acronym. Like all acronyms in a foreign language, the first step to understanding them is to realize that the new thing you are hearing for the first time is, in fact, an acronym and not an odd-sounding word. If you hear that someone lives *dans une ashellem* you can waste considerable time looking for it in a dictionary. It is only when you have understood that you are dealing with letters, and not a strange word, that you can look it up and find out that HLM is short for *habitation à loyer modéré* or low-cost housing. I have never heard anyone use the expression in full: they just say of someone, "*Il habite dans une HLM.*" In fact, more commonly, people tend to say, *dans un HLM* which is incorrect as the indefinite article has to agree with the real word *habitation* which is feminine, and not with the letters, which could arguably be considered to be masculine.

JOURNAUX: The people of Britain adore their newspapers; the people of France, for reasons I cannot understand, like theirs considerably less. A simple check of the various circulation figures shows this to be true. In Britain, the *Mirror, the Sun*, and the *Daily Mail* each have circulations in excess of two million copies a day with the *Daily Express* and the *Telegraph* selling around a million each. That is a lot of newsprint. To the daily papers should be added, at least in London, the *Evening Standard*, which has a circulation of over 400,000. In France, the total number of all newspapers sold each day is less than the circulation of the *Sun*. For example, France's major newspaper *Le Monde* is the biggest seller but with a circulation of only 400,000. Second comes *Le Figaro*, which sells 370,000 copies a day. *Le Monde* is an odd newspaper. It comes out in the evening but is dated the following morning. Then there is *l'Équipe*, which is the third bestselling newspaper in France but is by far the most fun to read. It contains all manner of stories but exclusively relating to a single subject, that of sports. Other newspapers have sports supplements or sports pages, but *l'Équipe* has stories about nothing else.

LA: Here, we are talking about "la" the musical note, not *la* the definite article, nor yet *là* with the accent on the *a* which means "there." The French tonic scale does not go "doh, ray, me, fah, soh, la, ti, doh" like Julie Andrews taught us that it should. In France it goes "do, ré, mi, fa, sol, la, si, do," which must make the French version of the song quite odd. I only mention "la" in this context because of a fascinating fact: the French dialing tone is a perfect "la" or A. This is a handy thing to know if you ever want to tune a musical instrument and only have a telephone at hand.

NOMBRES: Writing words in French is hard enough for English writers because you have to do the accents over and under some of the letters. According to French friends, non-French people write accents in a funny way so that they are immediately recognizable as having been done by a foreigner. It has something to do with starting them from the wrong end. Or possibly, going in the wrong direction. But worse than accents is the problem of writing figures. For French ones, sevens, and nines are not like their English counterparts. Of course you knew that continental sevens are crossed, but the nines are odd in that they have tails which curl round more than English ones. But by far the oddest figures are handwritten ones. These have an angled bar at the top which makes them look like a tired and depressed seven. The faster French people write their ones, the bigger the droopy arm tends to get so that a badly written one can end up looking like a deformed *n*. There are tales of French doctors writing prescriptions for English tourists which led the tourist to take seven pills instead of one because of the bad writing. Even though I now cross my sevens, all my numbers still look decidedly un-French.

NUMÉROS DE TELEPHONE: In France you give the digits of your phone number in pairs, each pair being dictated as a two-digit number. This means that you don't say five eight, seven four, but fifty-eight, seventy-four, and so on. This wouldn't really be a problem if it weren't for the infernal French numbering system. Numbers in French are logical up until a certain point, which, oddly perhaps, is sixty-nine, after which logic goes out of the window. Up to sixty-nine the numbering corresponds to the English way with numbers for twenty, thirty, forty, and so on being based on the numbers for two, three, and four with a suffix being added to show that it is a multiple of ten. You then just attach the required numerals so that the French for forty-two is *quarante-deux*, sixty-five becoming *soixante-cinq*. All simple so far. Then we get to seventy, which, instead of being something logical like *septante*, is in fact *soixante-dix* or "sixty ten." Things then get worse fairly rapidly for, after plowing through a series of additions including the equivalent of sixty-twelve and sixty-nineteen—*soixante-douze* and *soixante-dix-neuf*—we reach a new mathematical plateau with the number for eighty. Here addition is abandoned in favor of multiplication, where eighty becomes *quatre-vingts* or "four twenties." The long climb up to a hundred includes both multiplication and addition with ninety-three being *quatre-vingt-treize* or "four twenties thirteen" and ninety-nine being the incredible *quatre-vingt-dix-neuf* or "four twenties ten nine." All this may explain why French people are better at arithmetic than the English. This peculiar counting method causes problems when a French person dictates his phone number to you. With an English phone number you can write down the digits as soon as you hear them. In France you have to wait for the end of each pair. If the number includes figures beginning with *soixante* or *quatre-vingts*, you can't start writing before you have heard the whole number. If you hear *soixante* . . . and immediately write a six you may have to change it to a seven if the number turns out to be *soixante-douze*. It is all very time consuming.

-o: It is time that another wild generalization is allowed: the French have a thing about abbreviations that end in *o*. While French people like nothing better than shortening a word, there are a whole series of words which, when shortened, end in *o*. Many of these are medical words and possibly reflect their habit of going to see specialized doctors at the drop of a hat. For example, if you have a skin problem, you go to a dermatologist or *dermatologue*, or, if you are a woman, you may go to a gynecologist or *gynécologue*. In either case, when talking about it, the patient would not use the proper word but would say that she had been *chez le dermato* or would go and *voir la gynéco*. In fact they would probably be regular visitors and thus call them *ma dermato* or *ma gynéco*. Away from things medical, abbreviations ending in *o* also crop up in the gym, where abdominal exercises that are properly known as *des exercises abdominales* are invariably referred to as *abdos*. This should not be confused with *ado*, which is a common abbreviation of the word *adolescent*. The habit even extends to the environment, where *les écologistes* are commonly called *les écolos*, people of the green persuasion being referred to as *très écolos*.

PRIMO, SECUNDO . . . : When making a series of points in an argument, the French occasionally start counting in Latin. This is quite surprising when you hear it for the first time. Instead of saying *premièrement* for "firstly" they will prefix their first important point with the word *primo*. In the unlikely event that they don't get interrupted and manage to get to the second and third points, these should be prefixed by *secundo* and *tertio*, respectively. However, while people generally start off correctly, they often go wrong later on. } Thus, the second point often becomes *deuxio* instead of *secundo* presumably as a corruption of the word *deux*.

SOMMIER: This is a sneaky word whose existence I had never imagined until the day I first went to buy a bed in France. *Un sommier* can best be defined as the bit of the bed you didn't know you had to buy. I have looked it up in a French-English dictionary but there doesn't appear to be a translation for it. It is a word you learn when you are in a state of extreme weakness. You have wandered round a bed shop, increasingly troubled by the cost of the things, until you have at last found one that more or less meets your requirements. Of course, you had realized that the mattress would be sold separately, but had somehow imagined that the price you see attached to the rest of the bed itself would cover all you needed to buy. Think again, because there are in fact two labels attached to the bed. One for a sizeable sum which turns out to cover the bed itself—the bit you can see when you walk into the bedroom—and a second, for a lesser amount which appears to relate to *le sommier*.

This, you at last discover, is the wooden frame part that sits inside the bed and holds up the mattress. Why it is sold separately is beyond me. The bed simply isn't a bed without it because the mattress would end up on the floor. I have never bought a bed in the U.K. and thus have no idea whether such sneaky behavior is peculiar to France.

SUPPOSITOIRE: The list of things that might make you stop and think twice about coming to spend some time in France must include *les suppositoires.* (Those of a sensitive disposition should perhaps move quickly on to the next paragraph at this point.) In my sheltered youth, i.e., that part that was spent happily in England, I had never considered suppositories as a serious means of medication. My first contact with them was when looking through my parents-in-law's bathroom cabinet in search of aspirin. The search revealed a packet claiming to deal with *maux de têtes*, or headaches, that seemed promising. Opening the packet revealed the most surprising objects that I had ever seen in or outside a bathroom. Discreet questions were answered with an alarmingly unambiguous gesture explaining where such products were intended to be inserted. A reply along the lines of "Good heavens! But I'm English" led to mockery and ridicule. "*Mais, c'est très efficace,*" I was assured, but to no avail. But I think we should leave this subject here. And there is no way that I am going to discuss French thermometers, apart from relating the drama that arose in an Oxford boarding school where my wife was briefly a matron responsible for the health of a dozen eleven-year-old boys. One poor kid was traumatized for life when, on complaining that he had a temperature, he was pursued around the house by a French girl with a thermometer who demanded that he remove his shorts *tout de suite*.

SYNDIC/SYNDICAT: Confusion arose because I thought that one of these was the abbreviation of the other. The error came to light when I couldn't understand why our residents' association should be run by a trade union. For *un syndicat* is the French word for "trade union." The three principal trade unions in France are all known by their initials: you have FO (Force Ouvrière), CGT (whatever), and CFDT (whatever, too), whose representatives regularly appear on the news programs announcing future strikes or justifying previous ones. *Un syndic*, on the other hand, is the name for the management committee that runs the day-to-day affairs of an apartment building or other collective dwelling. You turn to *le syndic* when you think the heating should be switched on early, or when you want to know whether you are allowed to put up a satellite dish, or when you want to complain about your neighbor's dog. *Le syndic* also organizes the annual *réunion des copropriétaires* as the residents' annual general meeting is known. This is a dreadful affair that lasts for hours and involves voting on topics both important and unimportant. They are also the occasions where older residents get to speak at length in public for the only time in the year, as well as giving residents the opportunity to exact public vengeance on anyone who has caused offense since the last meeting.

VIRGULE: We have encountered all sorts of surprising things relating to French vocabulary, but there are even surprises in French when it comes to math. The most astonishing thing is the fact that a simple decimal point is not universal. I happily translated "two point five" as *deux point cinq* in the first weeks I lived in France because it never occurred to me that anyone might use anything other than a decimal point. But of course they do. The point between the integer and the decimal fraction is not a point but a comma in France. Thus, French people say *deux virgule cinq*. This is something that should be taken into account each time you write a check because fifteen euros and thirty centimes is 15,30 and not 15.30 (which, in France, is half past three). When you write big numbers in English, like fifteen thousand four hundred and ten, you would write 15,410. The French maintain their way of inverting commas and points by writing 15.410. Thus, a check for a large number would have something like 15.410,65 instead of 15,410.65.

$\mathscr{T}$HE BUSINESS WORLD

So, after reading all the preceding sections, and learning all the words, you must be thinking, "But, how can I get a job in France?"

We shall therefore finish with a selection of words covering how to get a job, and all the wonderful things that you will discover once you have one.

Getting *a* Job

BOSSER: No one actually works in France. By this I mean that no one uses the verb *travailler* to describe whatever activity they do while at their employer's place of business. This activity is invariably described instead by the slang verb *bosser*. The word manages to imply that the work being done is strenuous, tiring, or difficult; doing something nice, that you actually enjoy, would never be defined as *bosser*. After a long, tiring week, you might collapse at home with the words, *"C'est fou ce que j'ai bossé cette semaine."* Work itself—strictly *le travail*—has its own slang term, which is *le boulot*. This can cover the job—*"Qu'est-ce que tu fais comme boulot?"*—or the quantity of work that you have to do—*"J'ai énormément de boulot à faire aujourd'hui."* You can also use *bosser* for intellectual work such as studying for an exam, an activity that could be described with *Il faut que je bosse mon examen*, while studying your Spanish would be *bosser mon espagnol*.

CEDEX: This is a word that you often see at the end of a business address on an envelope, not so much when you are writing to a big company or a private firm, but more when you are writing to an organization that expects to receive a lot of mail that they need to deal with rapidly. Cedex stands for *Courrier d'Entreprise à Distribution Exceptionnelle*—or special delivery for business letters. In fact, in order to be sure of receiving their letters early in the morning, the company has to go to fetch the letters from the post office rather than waiting for the postman to deliver them. Experience shows that, just because a company has a Cedex address, they are no more likely to reply promptly to your letter than any other company.

FORMULES DE POLITESSE: This is the French equivalent of the English "yours truly" or "yours sincerely," which you put at the end of a formal letter. Unfortunately, whereas two words are perfectly sufficient in English, the French have a positively feudal attitude to finishing letters, preferring to use long-winded and ornate phrases which vary as a function of the person who is being written to. Just to give you an example, at the end of a letter where, in English, you would simply put "yours faithfully," a Frenchman would be expected to write, "*Je vous prie d'agréer, messieurs, l'assurance de mes sentiments distingués*." This roughly translates as the writer begging the reader to accept the assurance of his distinguished feelings. I mean really! Can you imagine asking the man from the electricity company to accept the assurance of your distinguished feelings? Or worse, what he might do if you did?

It doesn't stop there. If you are writing to a business-

man whom you know, you would finish your letter by saying, "*Je vous prie de croire, cher monsieur, à l'assurance de mes
salutations distinguées*," by which you would be asking him
to believe in the assurance of your distinguished salutations. How could you possibly know whether he believed
them or not, and how would it matter if he did? But when
it comes to writing to women, the French become unchar-
acteristically prudish. Finishing a letter to a woman with
any reference to feelings is considered unacceptable for
fear, presumably, of inflaming the poor creature's passions.
Therefore, in order to preserve her dignity, one is expected
to close a letter to a woman with the words, "*Je vous prie
d'accepter, madame, l'expression de mes respectueux hommages*."
This is guaranteed not to inflame anyone's passions as you
are merely asking her to accept the expression of your re-
spectful homage. This is unlikely to catch on in English
speaking countries or become a successful chat-up line.

LETTRE DE MOTIVATION: You can't just write and apply
for a job in France. Writing a simple cover letter as you
would in English, something along the lines of "I am writing to apply for the position advertised in the Oxford *Mail*
dated . . ." would be completely unacceptable in France.
You have to write *une lettre de motivation* or your chances
of getting an interview will be zero. This is the most syco-
phantic, hypocritical affair, which has to include phrases
like *votre annonce a retenu toute mon attention*—your advert
had me really gripped (well, something like that) as well as
declarations of overwhelming enthusiasm for the job and

the company, not to mention your desire to work for them until retirement, if not beyond. Needless to say, such letters are quite tough to write. There is therefore a strong market for books that set out various standard forms of letter that you can adapt to suit your own situation. Having been on the receiving end, as well as the sending end, of such letters, I view the whole thing as a waste of time. I selected those who would get an interview as a function of my wife's handwriting analysis of the letters, which is much more reliable.

PISTON, COPINAGE: There must be some conclusion that you can draw about the way things work in France from the fact that they have two common words for something that requires a whole expression to explain in English. We talk about having "friends in high places" or "knowing someone who can pull strings." The French have the word *piston*. If you aren't good enough to achieve something on your own, you need *piston*. This is the sort of help that comes from knowing someone important or from being the nephew of the managing director. Whoever it is will then exert their influence in your favor and the job or the promotion is yours, whether you deserved it or not. Your new colleagues will mutter darkly to each other that you got the job *par piston* or that you were *pistonné*. The mutterings will be an interesting mix of contempt blended with jealousy that they don't know anyone useful to help them. It's quite a relief to be English in France because I don't know anyone remotely useful and so no one can ever accuse me of being *pistonné* even though there are times when it might have been useful! The other word for this kind of help is *copinage*, which tends to refer to help that you get specifically from friends or from those who have been to the same GRANDE ÉCOLE as you.

Having *Got* the Job

CHÈQUES DÉJEUNER: These are luncheon vouchers given out in some offices in France. Their existence came to light on my very first morning in my first French office. A distinguished-looking lady appeared in my office carrying a small booklet. These she announced were *chèques déjeuner*, pointing out that there was one for each working day of that month, and that each was for a value of twenty francs. (This was many years ago.) When I enthusiastically stretched out my hand for this unexpected present, she firmly asked me for a check for two hundred francs. It took a while for me to discover what was going on. In France, spending on meals is considered a joint event between the employer and the employee with each contributing half the cost of the meal. Thus, although each check was for a nominal twenty francs, the company only paid ten francs, the other ten francs being paid in advance by the employee. Even at the time, it was very difficult to eat at lunchtime in central Paris for only twenty francs. When a company has an in-house cafeteria, the employer still contributes toward the cost of the meal, but this is in the form of subsidies that are invisible to the employee rather than *chèques déjeuner*.

COMITÉ D'ENTREPRISE: At last something that is much better in France: *le comité d'entreprise* of a large company is the equivalent of a social club writ large. French employment law states that every company with fifty or more employees must have such a club and specifies that it must receive one percent of the total of the company's salaries as a budget. This means that for a large company, the *comité d'entreprise* has some fairly serious spending power. What does it do with all this money? The *comité d'entreprise* funds all the various clubs and associations that are organized for the employees. It organizes vacation packages, which are offered at rates well below cost. As the packages are so cheap, the line to sign up usually starts to form very early in the morning. The social club also makes block bookings for concerts and plays and then subsidizes part of the cost of the ticket. In some companies, there are company sports clubs with tennis courts and swimming pools, the running of which is dealt with, and financed, by the *comité d'entreprise*. In other companies they choose to subsidize more of the cost of meals served at the cafeteria. The advantages for the employees are numerous, but the cost to the employer is high, which is why some companies carefully arrange not to go above forty-nine employees. It is, however, claimed that the social clubs of some huge companies, notably the French Electricity Company, EdF, have over fifty employees to handle all the social affairs (and the associated enormous budget) and so the social club has its own sub-social club.

IMPÔTS: *Les impôts* is a term which casts a chill into the strongest French heart. It means "income tax." The French do not like paying income tax and particularly do not like filling in their tax form each year. The tax form is commonly, and incorrectly, known as *la déclaration des impôts* (it should be called *la déclaration des revenues*, as you declare your earnings, not your tax.) This pastel-colored, deceptively friendly looking form drops through the letterbox each year in mid April. You then have until the end of May to fill it in and send it back. Once you have filled in your tax declaration, you can then participate in one of France's great annual events, namely sticking your tax form in the letterbox outside the tax building on the last possible day. As no one enjoys filling in their form, everyone leaves it to the very last minute. In order to be sure of it arriving on time, most people then decide to drive round to the tax center late in the evening and deliver their envelope by hand. Unfortunately, as everyone has had the same idea, you are faced with huge traffic jams in the area with uptight and stressed *contribuables*—taxpayers—tooting their horns furiously. I therefore generally abandon the car some streets away and walk the last few hundred meters. However, once you arrive at the door of the tax building, you are faced with another problem. As everyone else has already put their envelope in the letterbox, it is full to overflowing. Last time this happened I didn't want to leave my envelope sticking out of the letterbox where it might blow away or get pinched, so I pulled out a huge handful of other peoples' envelopes and shoved mine well down inside the box before roughly pushing the other envelopes back in place. I then walked back to the car worrying that someone else might do the same thing. This year I am going to send my form in by post.

INFORMATIQUE: It is a sign of how long I have been living in France that word processors and PCs appeared since I first arrived. I have thus learned the little I know about using Windows software in French and got used to saying *copier coller* long before I could cut and paste. In case you ever have to use a French computer when on holiday, for example when in an Internet café in France, a few basic terms might be of use. For a start, the Word toolbar which in the English version reads:

File, Edit, View, Insert, Format, Tool, Table, Window

says on my computer:

Fichier, Édition, Affichage, Insertion, Format, Outils, Tableau, Fenêtre.

A mouse is *une souris* while a mousepad is *un tapis de souris*. *Un clic droit* gives you the choice between *copier, couper et coller*. And *un fichier et un dossier* correspond to a file and a folder.

ORDINATEUR: In days gone by, when a brand-new device appeared on French soil, the French government and l'Académie Française insisted that whatever it was be given a French name rather than just adopting the English term. This was intended to preserve the French language. As far as I can see, the only time they really succeeded with this strategy was with the word for a computer, which is *un ordinateur*. This is a made-up word that was selected in place of the alternative *un computeur*. It has slipped into the French vocabulary quite happily. The same cannot be said for another made-up word that was supposed to become the generic name for personal stereos of which the forerunner was the Walkman. The Académie came up with the word *un balladeur* but this completely failed to gain popular support and is almost never heard. Everybody seems to call it *un Walkman*. Indeed, the only person I know who uses the word *balladeur* is me, purely out of cussedness. The current government seems to have given up the battle to retain French words for things because new terms such as USB, CD, and MP3 are used exclusively.

PONT: An excellent word in that it relates to days off at work. While in the U.K. and the U.S. public holidays invariably fall on a Monday, corresponding public holidays—of which there are a fair few—in France fall on a given date rather than on a given day of the week. Thus, each year, a public holiday shifts to a new day of the week. So, every so often, a public holiday will land on a Tuesday or a Thursday. This is where things get interesting. For the majority of employers, in an attempt to improve employee relations, will give the intervening Monday or Friday off as an extra holiday so as to bridge the gap, or *faire le pont*, between the public holiday and the weekend. In general, as soon as you receive next year's new diary, the first thing you will do is to check the days of the various public holidays and see how many *ponts* you are going to get. May is a wonderful month for *ponts* as there are three public holidays. In peak years, when everything falls perfectly you can get three long weekends. Whereas lots of companies used to give the extra day off, nowadays more and more are insisting that the days be taken out of your individual holiday allowance, especially that relating to flexible working. See RTT and VIADUC.

RTT: The French working week is very strictly defined. Some years ago, you had to work thirty-nine hours each week. This was real working hours and didn't include the lunch break. About twenty-five years ago, the working week was reduced to 37.5 hours. This is what I used to work when I first came to France and it meant a 7.5-hour working day. Then, the Socialist government came up with the brilliant idea of reducing still further the number of hours worked on the grounds that this would inspire employers to take on extra employees to do the work that was no longer being done by the existing employees. This was intended to reduce unemployment, though it is not clear that any new jobs were really created. What is clear is that RTT, which means *Réduction du Temps de Travail*, changed employees' lives immeasurably. Most companies decided that people should still do the same number of hours' work each week, because there was still the same number of things to do, but that the number of days off each year would be increased. The majority of employees received eleven extra days off a year. But rather than giving the days off freely, some employers require at least some of these days to be used for training purposes, and that the other days be used to make up long weekends—see PONT. Thus, RTT days would take the place of free days off that were previously given generously by the employer. Even allowing for that, there are still quite a few remaining days off. RTT has changed holiday traditions in France so that people now use their days off at odd times of the year to make up long weekends for short breaks away.

TREIZIÈME MOIS: This is a good term to learn if you work in France because it relates to bonus payments. When you attend a job interview and agree on your annual salary, you will typically learn that your salary will be divided into thirteen parts with one thirteenth paid each month, and the remaining thirteenth paid as a sort of annual bonus. In many companies, you get the thirteenth part just before Christmas so as to be able to squander it on presents. Other companies pay half the thirteenth month in July to help with summer vacation expenses, with the other half being paid in December. Clearly, these are not real bonuses: the extra payment was yours anyway; it has just been saved up for you by your employer. Some companies even divide your salary into fourteen or even fifteen parts and pay the extra bits at odd intervals throughout the year. Such companies are at the root of much jealousy among the ill-informed who are heard to mutter bitterly that so-and-so must be vastly wealthy because he earns fourteen months' pay a year. Clearly, it is your total annual salary that really counts, not the number of fractions that it is paid in. For some reason, my current employer divides my annual salary into twelve and a half parts with the extra half a month being paid in December.

VIADUC: We have learned the word PONT, which refers to an extra day off taken between a public holiday and the nearest weekend so as to provide a four-day break. When the public holiday falls on a Wednesday, some people take off two extra days, either at the beginning or at the end of the week, so as to have a really long break. By extension of the *pont* or "bridge" analogy, this is referred to as *un viaduc*.

And *Some* Acronyms to End on

ANPE: It is not the meaning of this acronym that is important—in fact it stands for *Agence Nationale Pour L'Emploi*, which is the French equivalent of a Job Center—it is just an example of the numerous French acronyms that start with an *a* but somehow sound as though they don't. The problem arises because, in practice, people say *l'ANPE* not *ANPE*. This means that you hear someone say that he is going for an appointment with the words *"Je vais à l'ANPE."* This, to the untutored ear, sounds just like saying, *"Je vais à la NPE."* If you haven't heard of the ANPE you may be fooled into looking up something called NPE which, of course, doesn't exist. This is probably not deliberate trickery on the part of the French, but one can never be sure. Similarly, unemployment benefits are called *l'Assedic* which, if you hear it for the first time, can fool you into thinking that you are dealing with the nonexistent *La Cédic*.

CAC 40: Pronounced "cack quarante," the Cac 40 is the French equivalent of a stock exchange share index. It stands for *Cotation Assistée en Continu* and comprises, as the name suggests, the share prices of the top forty French companies. As with other share indices, the CAC's health is widely reported, often in medical terms. When the economy is doing well, *le CAC se porte très bien*. Conversely, when shares are falling, *le CAC a passé une très mauvaise journée*. The Parisian stock exchange is known as La Bourse and is housed in an imposing building called Le Palais Brongniart, which sits in Place de la Bourse in the 2ème arrondissement. Incidentally, the top Parisian restaurants keep an eye on the CAC because they tend to have more customers when the index is rising.

SIGLE: *Un sigle* is an acronym—a set of letters that are used instead of a series of words. French acronyms aren't always as difficult as they first appear if you use the "try the letters another way around" strategy. If faced with TVA, you may not have any idea what it might stand for. But if you try the letters the other way around, you get VAT. If the words are generally similar, only the order will change as the adjectives are put after the subject. Thus, value added tax is *taxe à valeur ajoutée*. Similarly, while you might not recognize SIDA, changing the letters around gives AIDS, which is much more familiar. It doesn't always work, of course. The World Health Organization is *l'Organisation Mondiale de Santé*. Do what you will with OMS, you won't end up with WHO. Nevertheless, rather than giving up in despair at the sight of a French acronym, changing the letters round is often worth a try. Here—an easy one to start with! Have a go with the international organization known in France as l'OTAN.

Smic: Another acronym that is used as a noun. There is a strictly defined and regulated minimum wage in France and it is known as *le smic*. This means *"Le Salaire Minimum Interprofessionnel de Croissance."* It was created by law on January 2, 1970, and replaced something called *le smig* or *Salaire Minimum Interprofessionnel Garanti*. Interestingly, thirty-five years later, people still pronounce it SmiG rather than SmiC. When talking about jobs, notably for young people working part-time while in school, they will say, *"Il va toucher le smic"* or *"Il va être payer au smic."* Even though most people don't know what the *smic* currently is to the nearest euro per hour, they know it isn't much and that being paid it is not a good thing. Poor unfortu-nates who earn the *smic* for life are known as *smicards*. The amount of the *smic* is revised in line with inflation each July and currently stands at 8.03 euros per hour or 1217 euros per month.

$\mathscr{C}$ONCLUSION

Having lived for twenty years in France I think I am over the worst now. I have gone through that terrible time when I couldn't understand anything and reached a fairly happy state where I understand almost everything. Almost everything? Well, I don't think I will ever understand all the subtle jokes in a satirical political newspaper called *Le Canard Enchaîné*. But you can't have everything.

I have also found a way of dealing with the French while still remaining English. This is particularly important, especially when it comes to humor. My first attempts at humor in French all those years ago caused great confusion because I tried to be funny the English way. This means that I didn't laugh when I said something funny. Unfortunately, making a joke in French to a French person while not laughing is a risky business. As I wasn't laughing, the French person assumed that I didn't actually know that what I said was funny, and that I must have done it by accident. So, not only did he not laugh at my joke, but he actually tried helpfully to explain my own joke back to me. Believe me, the best way to kill a joke is to explain it back to the person who made it!

But I am over all that now.

You are luckier than me because you are able to learn from my unfortunate experiences. Now that you have read the book, you should be able to get to a more rewarding and enjoyable stage of visiting France a lot quicker than I did. You will thus be able to get more pleasure out of your next visit and feel that you are just that little bit more integrated in French life.

But please don't stop now, just because you have finished the book. Carry on taking an interest in French culture, even though it may require quite a bit of effort. You'll find you enjoy France even more if you do. And the French may well enjoy your visit more, too!

$\mathcal{A}$CKNOWLEDGMENTS

We have seen in the Introduction that I didn't know any of these words when I first came to France: a variety of long-suffering people had to teach them to me. So spare a thought for my first colleagues, those poor people who hadn't asked to have *"un anglais"* in their midst but who, thankfully for me, felt that *"un anglais"* who could speak a bit of French would be easier to have around than one who couldn't. So *"un grand merci"* goes to Jean and Gaby at SBB who did the groundwork in my spoken French as well as starting me on the dreadful stuff that you have to use in patents. Later on François and Marc at Elf took over and explained the subtleties and, among other things, put me off *"Par contre"* for life. Away from the office someone had to teach me the slang and all the others words you need to survive *"chez la belle famille."* For this thanks go to Inès, Anne, Marc, Valérie, Nathalie, and Eric.

On a more practical note, I would like to thank Jane Turnbull, Georgina Laycock, and Jessica Sindler, without whom I would have had to keep all these words to myself.

About the Author

Charles Timoney was born in Oxford, England, and has spent the past twenty-five years in France, where he works as a patent attorney. He lives outside of Paris with his wife, Inès, and their two children.